Praise for *The New Masculinity*

"Manley has written a practical, smart, and deep-hearted 'guide for unlearning.' An essential handbook for young people growing up in today's world, and men who feel lost within it."

—Sean Michaels, winner of the
2014 Scotiabank Giller Prize

"In reading *The New Masculinity*, I felt myself exhale for the first time in a long while. Alex's work shows deep empathy towards men while still holding them accountable for the ways they've caused harm. Healthier, kinder and stronger masculinities are possible and this book is the roadmap. It is essential reading."

—Julie S. Lalonde, author of *Resilience is Futile:
The Life and Death and Life of Julie S. Lalonde*

"Alex Manley's debut book *The New Masculinity* is a clarion call and guiding light for anyone wondering what a truly healthy, courageous vision of masculinity might look like in a historic moment when traditional—and 'toxic'—manhood has come increasingly under fire. A refreshing antidote to the snake-oil sellers and false 'gurus' peddling the same old patriarchal ideas that young men simply ought to double down on anger, toughness and self-reliance, *The New Masculinity* offers a vision of manhood that is courageous, compassionate and beautifully self-reflective."

—Kai Cheng Thom, author of *I Hope We Choose Love:
A Trans Girl's Notes from the End of the World*

"*The New Masculinity* is a helpful, well-researched roadmap for young men who want greater context about and understanding of where masculinity has been and where it's headed, given the changing gendered landscape."
—Andrew Reiner, author of *Better Boys, Better Men: The New Masculinity That Creates Greater Courage and Emotional Resiliency*

"*The New Masculinity* is an opportunity to think differently about what it means to be a man without insisting that masculinity is inherently bad, toxic or evil."
—Joanna Schroeder, writer and media critic, author of *Confronting Conspiracy Theories and Organized Bigotry at Home: A Guide for Parents & Caregivers*

THE NEW MAS CUL INI TY

A Roadmap for a 21st-Century Definition of Manhood

Alex Manley

Published by ECW Press
665 Gerrard Street East
Toronto, Ontario, Canada M4M 1Y2
416-694-3348 / info@ecwpress.com

Editor for the Press: Pia Singhal
Copy Editor: Jen Knoch
Cover design: Michel Vrana

LIBRARY AND ARCHIVES CANADA CATALOGUING IN PUBLICATION

Title: The new masculinity : a roadmap for a 21st century definition of manhood / Alex Manley.

Names: Manley, Alex (Poet), author.

Identifiers: Canadiana (print) 20220484120 | Canadiana (ebook) 20220484147

ISBN 978-1-77041-689-5 (softcover)
ISBN 978-1-77852-147-8 (ePub)
ISBN 978-1-77852-148-5 (PDF)
ISBN 978-1-77852-149-2 (Kindle)

Subjects: LCSH: Masculinity—Social aspects. | LCSH: Men—Identity. | LCSH: Sex role—Social aspects.

Classification: LCC HQ1090 .M36 2023 | DDC 305.31—dc23

This book is funded in part by the Government of Canada. *Ce livre est financé en partie par le gouvernement du Canada.* We acknowledge the support of the Canada Council for the Arts. *Nous remercions le Conseil des arts du Canada de son soutien.* We acknowledge the funding support of the Ontario Arts Council (OAC), an agency of the Government of Ontario. We also acknowledge the support of the Government of Ontario through the Ontario Book Publishing Tax Credit, and through Ontario Creates.

ONTARIO CREATES

ONTARIO ARTS COUNCIL
CONSEIL DES ARTS DE L'ONTARIO
an Ontario government agency
un organisme du gouvernement de l'Ontario

Canada Council   Conseil des arts
for the Arts   du Canada

Canada

PRINTED AND BOUND IN CANADA

PRINTING: MARQUIS   5 4 3 2

for Peter, my grandfather, who
taught my father how to be a man.
Because the things you showed him
helped him show me how to be myself.

Contents

what do men not do?

"We do a great disservice to boys in how we raise them. We stifle the humanity of boys. We define masculinity in a *very* narrow way. Masculinity is a hard, small cage, and we put boys inside this cage."

—Chimamanda Ngozi Adichie, *We Should All Be Feminists*

Let's start with something we can all agree on: masculinity is at what feels like a crisis point.

The #MeToo movement's explosion into the mainstream in 2017 pulled back the curtain on an epidemic of male sexual abuse long simmering beneath the surface of our culture.

As the drumbeat of gun violence intensifies with new mass shootings occurring daily in America,[1] the overwhelming maleness of the perpetrators—and the idea of "male mental health"—is sharpening into a piercing thing we ignore at our peril.

---

1   Sharon LaFraniere, Sarah Cohen and Richard A. Oppel Jr., "How Often Do Mass Shootings Occur? On Average, Every Day, Records Show," *New York Times*, December 2, 2015, https://www.nytimes.com/2015/12/03/us/how-often-do-mass-shootings-occur-on-average-every-day-records-show.html.

Meanwhile, educational outcomes for men and the percentage of men in school are both dropping fast,[2] and that's likely to have professional and financial outcomes too. Already, unhoused people and high school dropouts are overwhelmingly male. It's worth asking: what is going on with men right now?

If you ask men, there's a decent chance you'll get a response that frames the problem in vastly different terms. For many guys, traditional masculinity feels like it's under attack.

Feminism is on the rise and has been advancing the cause of women at home, in school, and in the workplace for well over a century. Terms like "mansplaining," "manspreading," "male privilege" and "toxic masculinity" are burrowing into mainstream thought. T-shirts claim that "The Future Is Female," and men are taking criticisms from all comers, from politicians to stand-up comedians to ads for diapers.

Meanwhile, the books people write about masculinity are called *The End of Men* and *The Time Has Come*. It can be hard not to feel like we're on the edge of something.

Hemmed in on all sides by a culture that's increasingly feminist and female-friendly, men today are caught between a model of masculinity no longer fully accepted by the world around them and a world around them for which they have no functioning model. Can they say hi to a woman on the street? Compliment her dress? Ask

_____

2   Derek Thompson, "Colleges Have a Guy Problem," *The Atlantic*, September 14, 2021, https://www.theatlantic.com/ideas/archive/2021/09/young-men-college-decline-gender-gap-higher-education/620066/.

her for her number? Slide into her DMs? Or will they get sneered at, yelled at, cancelled?

For some, the answers to these questions are obvious, but for many men they are pressing and profoundly anxiety-producing, and that anxiety has consequences. Left unchecked, it tends to push men towards another feeling: anger. In droves, men are turning to prophets of hate— sexist and racist men who promise that their salvation lies in doubling down on what the headlines are calling "toxic masculinity."[3]

Male-oriented publications, from the legacy ones like *GQ* and *Esquire* to often short-lived neo-men's mags like Deadspin's *Adequate Man* and *New York Magazine*'s *Beta Male* to viral-friendly online destinations like UNILAD, are often nominally about helping men better themselves. But they have been little help when it comes to stemming the tide of male anger, and academic-penned books about masculinity are often descriptive rather than prescriptive. They may manage to identify the problem, but the solution seems to be a lot slipperier.

To solve this problem, we need to understand its parts. We need to consider men, and masculinity, not just as a law of nature, the backdrop against which we live our lives, but treat them as an object of study.

So. What are men?

---

3 It's a term that I try to avoid using in this book, for a number of reasons. Though I believe much of modern masculinity is toxic in some way, I believe that many guys, hearing the term, believe that it implies that masculinity is *inherently* toxic, rather than describing, as the term was supposed to, a toxic version of masculinity that proliferates in our culture.

They're a section of the population that commits the overwhelming majority of rapes.[4] The overwhelming majority of murders.[5] The overwhelming majority of arson.[6] The overwhelming majority of violent crime, period.[7] They're behind more car crashes,[8] more bank robberies,[9] more fistfights.[10] As a group, they are dangerous and they live dangerously.

If men were any other group—a race, a religion, a linguistic group, a nationality, anything—and acted like this, it's hard to imagine them getting the kind of even-handed and preferential treatment they benefit from today. The truth is, for all the fear-mongering xenophobes like to

4   Adam Cotter and Laura Savage, "Gender-based violence and unwanted sexual behaviour in Canada, 2018: Initial findings from the Survey of Safety in Public and Private Spaces," Statistics Canada, December 5, 2019, https://www150.statcan.gc.ca/n1/pub/85-002-x/2019001/article/00017-eng.htm.
5   United Nations, "Global study on homicide: 2019 Edition," 2019, https://www.unodc.org/unodc/en/data-and-analysis/global-study-on-homicide.html.
6   Federal Bureau of Investigation, "2019 Crime in the United States," https://ucr.fbi.gov/crime-in-the-u.s/2019/crime-in-the-u.s.-2019/tables/table-42.
7   Ibid.
8   Nicholas Bakalar, "Behind the Wheel, Women Are Safer Drivers Than Men," *New York Times*, April 27, 2020, https://www.nytimes.com/2020/04/27/well/live/car-accidents-deaths-men-women.html.
9   Federal Bureau of Investigation, "Bank Crime Statistics 2020," https://www.fbi.gov/file-repository/bank-crime-statistics-2020.pdf/view.
10   Emily Chung, "Men's faces evolved to be punched, study suggests," CBC News, June 10, 2014, https://www.cbc.ca/news/science/men-s-faces-evolved-to-be-punched-study-suggests-1.2670756.

do about immigrants, queer people or people of colour, the really dangerous group is men. If this belief system were a religion, it would be derided as an ideology of hate—one with well over three billion adherents.

In the opening sentence of Liz Plank's 2019 book, *For the Love of Men*, she drops a hammer blow: "there is no greater threat to humankind than our current definitions of masculinity." She proceeds to make a solid case for the argument: the roots of contemporary masculinity are snaky and thick—they find their ways into economic crashes, wars, ecological disasters.[11]

They used to say "cherchez la femme" about the propensity of noir films to use a beautiful woman as the source of all the trouble, but in real life, it's the reverse—look for something going wrong on a mass scale and who's behind it? It's almost always a man, or, more likely, a large group of men.

Male-dominated boardrooms greenlight layoffs, male-led governments kick off armed conflicts, male-staffed companies destroy the planet's natural resources. If men hold the power all over the world, and the world is in turmoil, it's worth asking: what if that's not a coincidence?

~

If you're a man reading this, you're probably not one of those boardroom execs sending men to strip-mine the world, or firing them when they've outlived their

11   Liz Plank, *For the Love of Men: A New Vision for Mindful Masculinity* (New York: St. Martin's, 2019).

usefulness. You're likely not one of the government officials pulling the trigger on a war.

You're probably closer to the other guy: the man in the mine, or the man who got fired, or the man in the trenches. You're probably wondering what the hell you did to get lumped in with those assholes ruining the world. You're just making your way through life—going to school, or work, trying to scrape together a living, talking to your friends, fantasizing about your crushes, gaming to blow off steam. Maybe you feel fine about being a man or maybe you don't, but you're not stupid. You've noticed, one way or another, that masculinity isn't as popular today as it used to be.

It snuck up on us. There wasn't a big ceremony, like sending smoke into the sky to signify that they've chosen a new pope. There wasn't some sort of update or algorithm change, like when a social media platform suddenly looks different one morning.

Instead, it happened in pieces. There was a screenshot of a tweet somewhere trash-talking men that got 50,000 retweets. Every week, some celebrity was losing his job. A flirty message gets a block or an unmatch instead of a response. At some point someone said men can't even open doors for women anymore. Chivalry's not just dead, you might conclude—it's been murdered by man-hating feminists. And god forbid you voice a thought like that aloud around the wrong person, or you'd be the very next one getting cancelled.

If you're feeling testy lately, you're not imagining it. There was no all-caps neon-sign warning, but things have, in fact, changed. Men are being given shorter and shorter leashes. It's not cool to ogle at and drool over beautiful naked bodies anymore—unless it's a man's body. It's not cool to brag about kicking a one-night stand out of your apartment—unless it's a man getting shoved into the street. It's not cool to make sexist jokes anymore—unless a man is the butt of the joke. There men are, in sitcoms, stand-up routines, TV commercials, viral posts: the butt of the joke, again and again and again. If you're a man, you could be forgiven for getting tired of it all.

To some guys, it might seem like there are really only two options these days: you pretend you don't notice it, or you get angry. Lots of guys pretend they don't, and they're doing alright. Their lives haven't been too shaken up by all the changes. Maybe they're self-proclaimed feminists, maybe they're too rich to care, maybe they always got along better with women, maybe they really love their mom, maybe their girlfriend is outspoken, maybe they're gay.

But if you're one of the guys getting angry, that might have consequences. It's hard to feel angry about this kind of thing without it leading somewhere. When you try to express your confusion, you're met with blank stares. People laugh awkwardly or change the subject. People debate you in earnest, then call you a bigot. So you seek out people who understand you, or seem to, at least. And that's how guys fall in with the wrong crowd.

If you're looking to recruit an army, offer them an alternative. The corners of the internet where people go to talk about how angry they are aren't elite places. The barrier to entry is low. They want you to join—they want you to feel welcome there, along with them, stewing in anger. And maybe that's all it is—a place to vent with like-minded people. But usually it's not.

There are real people who were radicalized on sites and message boards like these, who've used real guns to murder other real people. That might sound like broadcast news jargon, but "radicalized" isn't a made-up concept. It means you've had your worldview become more and more angry, less and less tethered to society, and you've become more and more willing to become violent. This kind of thing happens online with terrifying regularity.[12] What we read and who we talk to changes us. And some people become so changed, so honed over time into something brittle and sharp, like an arrowhead—that they open up to the idea of killing.

A young man in 2014, in Isla Vista, California, for instance. Or one in Quebec City in 2017. Toronto, 2018. Christchurch, New Zealand, 2019. Buffalo, 2022. Killers who became radicalized online. Every one of them once a baby, someone family members cooed over, someone small and pudgy, exploring life, full of promise, and who then unravelled, slowly and then all at once, into a killing thing.

~

As much as you may not feel like you have any kinship with the bosses or the politicians I mentioned as being hallmarks of toxic masculinity earlier, you may not feel

12   Nora Saks and Ben Brock Johnson, "How to stop online extremism from becoming offline violence," WBUR, May 20, 2022, https://www.wbur.org/endlessthread/2022/05/20/online-platforms-buffalo-shooting.

like you have any kinship with the mass killers, either. But it's worth asking: what were these men who snapped so angry about? Their own lives, ruined? Presidents and billionaires swathed in power and prestige while these future shooters were crushed underfoot? Unjust policies that stole from the poor and gave to the rich?

No. They targeted people they saw as weaker than them: women, people of colour, queer people, immigrants. They saw their power waning and lashed out at the people they perceived in the rear-view mirror. They are an extreme example of an anger that so many men feel these days, an anger that seems to swallow more men every passing year. They want to know where their power, their status, their dominance went.

You don't need to be a scholar of empire to know that members of a dominant social class often mistake a particular set of socio-historical circumstances for an objective, universal truth. When you're on top for a long time, it's easy to feel like it's the natural order and will last forever.

But that's not how empires work. The Incan, Roman and British empires fell. The American one is falling as you read this.

And the dominance of men is crumbling too.

Now, women represent the majority of college graduates, and that number is only climbing.[13] With jobs that

13   Kim Parker, "What's behind the growing gap between men and women in college completion?" Pew Research Center, November 8, 2021, https://www.pewresearch.org/fact-tank/2021/11/08/whats -behind-the-growing-gap-between-men-and-women-in-college -completion/.

favor traditionally masculine skills increasingly being automated out of existence, as I'll explore more in Chapter 13, women's higher education and stranglehold on so-called soft skills like kindness and "human interaction" presents men with a powerful conundrum.

And, because man-first false equivalencies like "When's International Men's Day?" and "Men suffer from domestic abuse, too," have for so long been the province of chauvinists and misogynists, it's hard to take seriously the idea that men are on the precipice of actual extinction.

Women, having borne the brunt of male violence, anger and discrimination for millennia, aren't about to let their foot off the gas just as they're coming into their own.

Complaints that boys are hard done by in school when asked to participate in more girl-friendly curriculums are met with laughter by women whose academic experiences were rife with unwanted attention from creepy profs, restrictive dress codes and sexual bullying. Complaints that men make up the bulk of low-status and dangerous jobs like garbage collectors and lumber workers are met with reminders that women get paid less for the same work across all sectors,[14] and, as I'll explore more in Chapter 2, often aren't paid at all.

---

14   Amanda Barroso and Anna Brown, "Gender pay gap in U.S. held steady in 2020," Pew Research Center, May 25, 2021, https://www.pewresearch.org/fact-tank/2021/05/25/gender-pay-gap-facts/.
    Robin Bleiweis, "Quick Facts About the Gender Wage Gap," American Progress, March 24, 2020, https://www.americanprogress.org/article/quick-facts-gender-wage-gap/.
    Joe McCarthy, "What Is the Gender Pay Gap and How Do We Close It?" Global Citizen, March 11, 2021, https://www.globalcitizen.org/en/content/what-is-the-gender-pay-gap/.

I'll be honest: the sexist men who inhabit the worst corners of the internet's shady underbelly are right about one thing. The gender revolution is upon us, and it won't be kind to men. They're wrong about just about everything else, though. And it's worth remembering, when considering all this, how women got to where they are. It wasn't by sticking to what they were told was the right way to be a woman. It was by being forward-thinking, justice-oriented, and united. There's a lesson there for men who are wondering how to be men in the 21st century—a group of people who are, broadly speaking, confused about their role in society going forward, nostalgic for a past that's not coming back, angry to the point of cruelty and splintered into factions.

So what do you do when you're on a sinking ship? Traditional masculinity holds that the captain goes down with it. And you can cosplay as a ship captain if you want, but for my money, the smart move is to get the hell off the sucker.

What I'm proposing isn't that men stop being men entirely. I'm not suggesting widespread self-inflicted genital mutilation or the mandatory wearing of pink dresses—although, if that second one is something you've been considering, go for it. But the reason it's not what I'm suggesting is because that's not what I or most people want out of men.

Often, people who've experienced a certain privilege all their lives overreact when they lose a little bit of it. People who've never been publicly criticized for their actions before call a few negative online comments a "lynch mob" or a "witch hunt," when usually their status and careers are never especially in question, let alone their actual lives and physical safety. What we're seeing now is not a war on men, but rather, a shift—some pushback. If there was a war on men, women and queer people would be killing men every single day. But that's simply not happening. (Instead, as I'll explore more in Chapter 8, it's exactly the inverse.)

Because at the end of the day, whether they're trans or non-binary people or cis women, almost all people who aren't men do love men. They love their fathers, their sons, their brothers, their uncles, their cousins, their grandfathers; their husbands, their boyfriends, their lovers; their friends, their coworkers, their neighbours, their colleagues, their favourite artists and athletes. So when straight women lament how annoying men are, what they're secretly saying is: I wish I could quit you. But I can't. And the queer community loves men too—when someone comes out as a trans man, it's cause for celebration. If masculinity itself was the enemy, these people would be excommunicated. But they aren't.

The enemy isn't men—it's the toxicity that exists within traditional masculinity. Your family members, dating app matches, classmates and coworkers don't want eunuchs, they just want considerate, caring humans that they can feel confident won't ruin their lives, won't become violent, possessive or cruel.

We make our way there collectively by building a new vision of what men are and can be that's not weighed down by the baggage of the stories we've been telling ourselves about them this whole time. Because stories about masculinity are spoon-fed to all of us as we grow up, and those beliefs impact people regardless of their gender. These narratives and ideologies influence things like what you expect of the men around you and how people alter themselves and their behaviour to fit around men. These stories help shape what and who men are. And as I'll explore time and again throughout this book, we underestimate the power of stories at our own peril.

~

I came to be conscious of maleness at a young age. It's hard not to when your last name is a homonym for the adjective most people associate with men. If your last name is Mann, or if it rhymes with "macho" or "masculine," maybe you understand.

The kids I went to school with couldn't help themselves. To them, I was Alex Girley, Alex Womanley, Alex Unmanley, Alex Not-So-Manley. I wasn't especially tall until late in my teens, was always pretty skinny, not muscular and had very little body or facial hair. I wasn't the strapping lumberjack type, the popular jock or even the class clown. I was a dorky nerd. But I ended up riding that dorky, nerdy quality all the way to my first job out of university—working for the website AskMen.com.

Founded in 1999 in my hometown of Montreal, Quebec, when I worked there, AskMen boasted that it was "the world's No. 1 lifestyle site for men." While it had offices in New York, London and Sydney, its headquarters were situated on the eighth floor of an office building in Montreal's charming Plateau neighbourhood, and inside, the place felt like a stereotypical website office—white walls, glass doors, open concept, free snacks. Though by 2018 the same space would feel like a ghost town, with a skeleton crew keeping things running and half the desks carted away, in 2013 it was exciting to feel myself amid the hustle and bustle of a 30- to 40-person crowd day in and day out, all of us focused on making content in one way or another, under the banner of the site's slogan: "Become a Better Man."

I was only a few months into that feeling of excitement when Jake, one of the managers, revealed the whole nature of the operation in a sentence or two. So often, that kind of prized knowledge is something you have to earn access to over years and years of toil. They don't hand out a laminated sheet with the recipe to the secret sauce when you first get hired. I was 25, and this was my first job that didn't involve a cash register. I was working as a copy editor—the person responsible for checking the articles we published for mistakes, typos and assorted screw-ups. I was essentially the bottom of the organizational ladder, just one rung up from an unpaid intern.

So why was Jake, who managed the site's video content and wore popped-collar polos, showing me what lay behind the curtain? The truth is, it was an accident. Not that he told me accidentally; it was a very intentional admission. The accidental part of it was that he didn't seem to realize what he was saying was so important, that it was the foundational ethos of not only our entire company, but the very concept of men's publishing as it existed at the time, and, frankly, much of what we consider masculinity itself, even to this day.

I'd been talking to Jake—like almost every other person I'll mention in this book, Jake is not his real name, but it fits him well enough—about headline strategy, something much discussed within the digital publishing industry, and little outside of it, apart from when people make fun of clickbait-style headline formats that have become too popular. That's when he revealed the truth to me—an unwritten rule for the videos his employees produced, he said, and a tactic that had been finding its way into the headlines I'd been writing for much of my time at the company, without my having consciously realized it.

"We just try to scare 'em," Jake said. "The fear makes them click."

What Jake had discovered, whether by trial and error or out of some innate understanding of the fragility inherent to masculinity, was that headlines that implied the reader was doing something wrong, had something wrong with him or was unforgivably unaware of something important seemed to get better results than those that didn't.

I kept on thinking about what Jake had revealed in the weeks and months following that brief exchange, and as the years went by it came to inform more and more of how I understood the business of publishing articles for men. People visit websites for all kinds of reasons, but the reason men visited ours was because they were afraid.

Lots of other things, of course, made men click—and thus, according to the financial logics of digital publishing, made us ad revenue—but nothing seemed to draw visitors to the site and its articles like the power of fear. The articles that performed the best, year after year, were articles that spoke to specific male fears, that offered information or advice on topics that men couldn't talk to their friends or their fathers about. Fear drove men.

It's hard to spend six years contemplating all that fear and not come to empathize with the scared people you're catering to. While the conversation around men was shifting under our feet, I recognized that men weren't the monsters they were often made out to be on social media. When they hurt people, which was often, it was too often because they'd been hurt themselves. They'd been raised wrong—by their parents, in some cases, but more often by the world around them. They'd been taught unhealthy lessons at every step of their journey, and now they were being blamed for the toxicity they'd ingested. And the rest of the world—women and queer people—had spent so much time feeling scared, annoyed or exhausted by men that they didn't seem to have any energy left for educating them.

What today's men need, I said to myself, is a how-to guide. Something to help them feel less afraid, less alone. Less lost.

~

In working on this book, I read something like 50 other books. Books that talked about men, boys, masculinity, gender, sex, violence. I was already well-read, and someone who'd been reading and writing articles about men and manliness for over a decade, but I hadn't ever had the time to sit down and really intentionally study the subject. (Whenever I'd heard gender studies discussed in the past, it seemed like it was code for women's studies, as though masculinity was the default, the ground against which other things emerge as figure.)

Each book was different, but they seemed to circle back to certain touchstones in interesting ways. They would bring up the Industrial Revolution, the rise of single-parent families, the 2014 Isla Vista shooting. They would touch on the work of the anthropologist Marija Gimbutas, name-drop specific African and/or Indigenous tribes and refer to the behaviour of chimpanzees and other primates. They would mention *Lord of the Flies* and the writing of the Russian masters Tolstoy and Dostoevsky, or the 20th-century socialist writers Hemingway and Orwell. They would mention Joseph Campbell's research into the structure of stories; they would find space for the theories of famous thinkers with German-sounding last names—Nietzsche and Freud, Jung and Marx. They would bring up the Boy Scouts, Hillary Clinton and Barack Obama. On occasion, these books would refer to each other—as I am doing here.

What they almost never did, though, was speak directly to boys and young men.

Collectively, regardless of the author's gender, these books were written for grown men, or adults, or parents of boys, or people who were interested in masculinity in an academic sense but not experiencing it firsthand, or vague, undefined audiences. Not one of them seemed interested in looking young men and boys in the eyes and walking them through anything. Not one of them seemed to aim to be part of a process of teaching them how to be men, though many of the books cried out for more of that very same thing in the world.

Part of the reason for that, of course, is that—as the thinking goes—teen boys and young men don't buy books, don't read, won't make money for the publishers. The book you're holding was turned down by dozens of publishing houses before it found a home, and almost all of them said the same thing: *This is a great idea. The world needs this book. Boys and young men need this book. But who's going to buy it?*

Yet these were the very same people who watched Jordan B. Peterson's *12 Rules for Life* skyrocket up the bestseller lists. Though none of the 12 rules of its title speaks directly about masculinity and its intended audience seems to be a general reader, upon closer inspection, that book reveals itself to be subtly (and at times not so subtly) aimed at a male audience. And how else to understand its success, if not for the fact that teen boys and young men very clearly do buy and read books, if only those books are *for* them?

Though men still occupy a disproportionate number of the very top jobs, the publishing industry is overwhelmingly populated by cis white women. I'm not saying that's necessarily a bad thing, in most cases—but even progressive, thoughtful and caring people have things they can't see, and the more everyone in the room looks like you, as I explore in Chapter 12, the more likely you'll miss things.

How can you properly cater to teen boys and young men if you've never been one and will never be one? So let me be clear: this is a book for teen boys and young men, because whether they were assigned male at birth or not, they're dealing with a world that's becoming less and less friendly to the visions of masculinity they've inherited.

If that's not who you are, I encourage you to keep reading too. If I've done my job right, there'll be something for everyone in this book's pages, and the same way women aren't the only people who can be feminists, men aren't the only people who can absorb and replicate traditional masculinity's toxic mentalities. Understanding the ways masculinity presents itself—and can heal itself—will be useful to people no matter their gender. But from my perspective, the people who most need a roadmap for how to be right now are the men of tomorrow.

Part of the problem, it strikes me, is that contemporary society features no real roles for teenage boys. They're rarely engaged in the wider culture in meaningful ways—confined to interactions with their peers, ignored or belittled by adults. In older cultures across the planet, from the not-too-distant past to the dawn of civilization, you'd be likely to find roles for young men; crucially, they'd be engaged in regular interactions with other community members, extended family members and so forth. There would be, as a number of men whose writing I read while researching this book have noted, other adult men in their lives, in a real and meaningful way, outside of their fathers. But in today's atomized, increasingly community-less society of North America, good male role models are hard to come by. Male teachers are a relative rarity and too overwhelmed by large class sizes and underfunding to play meaningful roles in all of their male students' lives. Fears—in some cases valid, in some cases less so—about male sexual predators have erected cultural walls between men and boys. Fatherhood is a fraught role, with low expectations and low investment compared to motherhood. If it takes a village to raise a child, too often women are the only ones participating. There's a masculinity void for young men, one that gets filled either horizontally, by the juvenile masculinity they see their peers model, or vertically, by the over-the-top masculinity they see modelled in the mass media. Neither is likely to teach them healthy lessons, either about how to be a man today or how to be a man tomorrow. So that's what this book is setting out to do.

~

Are you more manly, or more masculine?

If you're not sure which to answer, that's perfectly understandable. Though the two words originally were meant to indicate very different things, they've come to exist side-by-side in many people's lexical imaginations, in a stable that houses an agglomeration of male-oriented adjectives, along with stuff like "macho" and "John Wayne–esque."

But, as historian Gail Bederman explains in her book, *Manliness & Civilization*, people at the turn of the 20th century were under no such confusion. At the time, "manly" and "masculine" denoted vastly different traits and, as a corollary, vastly different men.[15]

Like so many things in our culture, there's a racist element to the divide—the terms, to some degree, existed to describe how white men saw themselves and how they saw men of colour. To be manly was a noble pursuit—to be in control of oneself. An orator, a thinker, a businessman, esteemed by his colleagues and contemporaries. To be masculine, however, was to be a savage—an animal, all brute force, muscle and instinct.

Depending on how you see the concept of a man, you might say that the manly man is truer to the ideals of manhood—or you might say that the masculine man is. What you can't say is that they're the same thing. One is about self-control, the other about its absence; one is about physical strength, the other about intellectual power.

That's not to say that this list of dialectics cannot be present in equal measure in the same body—just that here we have two markedly different conceptions of what it means to be a man, posed in diametrical opposition to each other.

It might seem strange that they've become synonymous with each other in recent decades, but, to my mind, it's just further proof that contemporary masculinity (or manliness) is a very confused ideology, without much by way of guiding principles.

The closest thing contemporary masculinity has to an overarching ethos is probably that it's an ideology of

15   Gail Bederman, *Manliness & Civilization: A Cultural History of Gender and Race in the United States, 1880–1917* (Chicago: University of Chicago Press, 1995).

negativity. That is, to be a man is to be defined not by what you *do* but by what you *don't* do. Journalist Peggy Orenstein, in her 2020 book, *Boys & Sex*, interviews dozens of college-age American males, and when asking them about their visions of maleness, discovered that many were constructed not from concrete attributes but from what wasn't being done.[16] So we get formulations like: Boys don't ____. Real men don't ____. Guys would never ____. It's against the bro code to even think of ____.

You don't need to be a masculinity scholar at a prestigious Ivy League institution to fill in those blanks. Most people—regardless of gender—can take a stab at them by the time they reach kindergarten, if not earlier; can place concepts and actions in and outside of what the masculinity expert and community organizer Jeff Perera calls the "Man Box." As Rachel Giese quotes Perera in her 2018 book, *Boys*: "the formula for manhood is the denial of everything perceived as soft, or gentle, or emotional or feminine."[17]

These dichotomies aren't just about choosing blue over pink in the maternity ward. They have consequences, and those consequences are life-and-death serious: American men die, on average, five years before women[18]. In fact,

16 Peggy Orenstein, *Boys & Sex: Young Men on Hookups, Love, Porn, Consent, and Navigating the New Masculinity* (New York: Harper, 2020).
17 Rachel Giese, *Boys: What It Means to Become a Man* (Toronto: Harper, 2018).
18 Sherry L. Murphy, B.S., Kenneth D. Kochanek, M.A., Jiaquan Xu, M.D., and Elizabeth Arias, Ph.D., "Mortality in the United States, 2020," NCHS Data Brief, December 2021, https://www.cdc.gov/nchs/data/databriefs/db427.pdf.

men die younger in almost every single country in the world.[19] People love to joke about stressful moments or bad habits taking years off their lives, but right there in front of us we have something that does that on a horrifyingly reliable basis: masculinity.

Men kill themselves more,[20] they die of medical conditions they avoid talking to doctors about,[21] they die from loneliness as they waste away in old age without a genuine social network.[22] But this is not just a case of men being the victims of their belief systems—the consequences of masculine ideology also spring outward from the self like a horrible tendril. When boys and men are cruel to other boys and men, they are weaving a web of pain: people who've been traumatized and hurt often go on to traumatize and hurt others. Violent crimes beget more violent crimes. It's an exhausting cycle.

I've written and edited for a men's website for close to a decade now, and I've seen how angry, scared and lonely men feel, how entrenched in a culture war they feel. So

19   United Nations, "Women outliving men 'everywhere', new UN health agency statistics report shows," April 4, 2019, https://news.un.org/en/story/2019/04/1036091.
20   American Foundation for Suicide Prevention, "Suicide statistics," https://afsp.org/suicide-statistics/.
21   T.J. Holwerda, A.T.F. Beekman, D.J.H. Deeg, M.L. Stek, T.G. van Tilburg, P.J. Visser, B. Schmand, C. Jonker, R.A. Schoevers, "Increased risk of mortality associated with social isolation in older men: only when feeling lonely? Results from the Amsterdam Study of the Elderly (AMSTEL)," Psychol Med., September 6, 2011, https://www.ncbi.nlm.nih.gov/pmc/articles/PMC1121551/.
22   Centers for Disease Control and Prevention, "Loneliness and Social Isolation," https://www.cdc.gov/aging/publications/features/lonely-older-adults.html.

many men would never even pick this book up, fearful of the apostasy hidden in its pages; if you've made it this far, consider yourself brave. What this book contains is a guide for unlearning. There are an infinite number of ways to be a person, but in order to access them in their fullness, you first need to unlearn the restrictions imposed on you by modern masculinity, the ways society has taught you to shave parts of yourself off until you're a man, not a human.

That's why I'm breaking this book down into sections based around things men don't do. You may never have been told not to do any of these things explicitly, but the culture you live in warns you off from each of them in different ways, some more and less subtle. And I believe behind each of those locked doors is a vision of the future—a new masculinity. So in each chapter, I'm going to make a case for why you should start doing exactly those things. Only once you've gotten comfortable doing the things men don't can you start being someone who's not hemmed in and hampered by the narrow, fragile masculinity you were spoon-fed growing up by your family, your friends and society at large.

So, here are 13 different things so-called "real" men don't do—and why you should break from the herd and get started on them as soon as you can.

1

~~a real man doesn't~~
get friendzoned

"Males as a group have and do benefit the most
from patriarchy, from the assumption that they are
superior to females and should rule over us. But
those benefits have come with a price. In return for
all the goodies men receive from patriarchy, they are
required to dominate women, to exploit and oppress
us, using violence if they must to keep patriarchy
intact. Most men find it difficult to be patriarchs. Most
men are disturbed by hatred and fear of women, by
male violence against women, even the men who
perpetuate this violence. But they fear letting go of
the benefits."

—bell hooks, *Feminism Is for Everybody*

I spent Valentine's Day 2005 working on my grade 11
science-fair project with the love of my life. I was 16;
she was 17; the project was about bacteria; and as we

sat in the corner of her parents' grey-carpeted basement, eating little candy hearts a 23-year-old banker had given her, I was so, so, so deep in the friendzone.

She—I'll call her Melissa—was an anomaly. Beautiful, smart, funny, popular—and she wanted to talk to me. I was a mess the way teenage boys are a mess—hair too long, clothes too baggy, face too oily, glasses too ugly.

I was a mess of contradictions too. Politically left, religiously devout, I listened to anti-authoritarian punk rock but spent my Friday nights at my church's youth group. I didn't fit in there, or anywhere; I considered myself fiercely countercultural, a lone warrior-poet, but I craved acceptance from the cool cliques I claimed to spurn.

Somehow, she didn't seem to mind that I didn't have anything going for me in the conventional sense. We'd fallen into talking every night on MSN Messenger after a mutual friend convinced me to work on the yearbook, which Melissa was helming. She was the type of girl who dabbled casually in the staples of teenagehood that I was too awkward and too shy to dare try my hand at—the dates, the house parties, the school dances, the underage drinking. That shimmering life where everyone was beautiful and no one was sad.

But when we talked online, we made sparks, like flint struck against steel. I saw her as an emissary, a golden angel from another realm sent down to me, but what she saw was someone whose relentless quick wit and dark sense of humour made for better conversations than all the cool kids she was used to chatting with. One day she asked me if I'd be her science-fair partner. I was in shock. It felt like someone was pranking me. But she meant it.

In the end, the bacteria project wasn't much to write home about. We were both good students, but we couldn't come up with any truly impressive ideas. Still, the conversations kept on flowing long after that year's science fair. Like the spots of bacteria we swabbed into clear plastic containers full of agar, the thing between us grew and grew. We became friends.

~

The problem most straight guys who can't get laid have with women is not that they can't get laid; it's that they have no idea what a woman is. "Incels," as many of them now self-identify, cobble together an image of women that's totally at odds with itself.

According to them, women are unattainable goddesses while simultaneously being nothing more than dirty sex objects. According to them, women are perfect-looking, makeup-caked frauds and liars, but also fat, ugly whores. And, according to them, women are dumb and incapable of valuable contributions to society, while at the same time deeply necessary to their happiness and the survival of the species.

In this constantly twisting tornado of a worldview, women are both the most and least important parts of their lives—cold-blooded sirens whose presence and company they eschew and slaver over in equal measure.

Apart from the horrifying misogyny of it all, what's most striking about all this posturing from the angry men in our culture—the incels, MGTOWs,[23] red-pill-eaters and various assorted bros—is that it seems like all of them have formed their ideas of women not based on what actual women are like but based on a dim, hazy view they've gleaned from a few chance encounters, supplemented by hearsay, rumour and the glossy gender lies of American pop culture.

To their credit, I'll grant them that pop culture has lied about women. The women they've watched on a screen have far too often been fabrications. They look ways most women don't look, sure, but too often they say and think and do things most women don't do and fall for men in ways most women don't fall—immediately, deeply, irrevocably.

(The ending, the complex work of the forever-after—that's elided, of course. No sense in letting details like life get in the way of a good story arc.)

Women in movies and TV are almost without fail speaking lines written by men, acting as characters dreamt up by men, being directed and shot and edited by men, selected for the role in the first place by men—the men who run the entertainment industry know these facts will fall away in comparison to a beautiful young woman's face. The media machine that's set up to tell these stories is well-oiled and powerful, with a formidable back catalogue to boot. Men grow up steeped in this culture of lies, of

_____

23   This stands for "Men Going Their Own Way," a sort of Reddit-associated separatist movement for men who decide they'd rather not interact with or rely on women at all.

holding women at arm's length, of the war of the sexes, where dates are missions into enemy territory.

By now, you may have heard of the Bechdel Test—that shorthand way of determining whether a movie does the bare minimum when it comes to its female characters. American cartoonist Alison Bechdel set out the rules in a 1985 comic strip, and to pass, a movie has at least two named female characters who have a conversation with each other about something other than a man. Lots of your favourite movies fail. Many have one or no women in them at all; some have women who aren't ever named or don't speak, many have two named women who never interact and some have their named female characters only onscreen to discuss the men in the story.

Like I said, passing the Bechdel Test is the bare minimum. Many of the films that do pass feature only conventionally attractive, white, cis, able-bodied women. The real worth of the Bechdel Test is its ability to show us the big picture, in seeing at a glance how Hollywood keeps making the same movies over and over, spending hundreds and hundreds of millions of dollars making movies without women, or movies where women don't speak, or movies where a single, impossible woman moves through seas of hulking men like an ornate tea cup being knocked about a giant bullpen. Movies where women are plot points, objects, Potemkin images, not people.

It's not that jarring to see onscreen women treated this way by filmmakers, because this is how real women are treated in real life by real men: Like they aren't real. Like they don't matter. Like they're just there to prop up the fiction, to fill things out.

In her famous 1929 polemic, *A Room of One's Own*, the British author Virginia Woolf explores the issue by inverting the dynamic: "Suppose, for instance, that men were only represented in literature as the lovers of women, and were never the friends of men, soldiers, thinkers, dreamers; how few parts in the plays of Shakespeare could be allotted to them; how literature would suffer! We might perhaps have most of Othello; and a good deal of Antony; but no Caesar, no Brutus, no Hamlet, no Lear, no Jaques — literature would be incredibly impoverished, as indeed literature is impoverished beyond our counting by the doors that have been shut upon women."[24]

In video games, the characters there to fill out the fiction are called NPCs. Non-player characters. You are the protagonist. They are two-dimensional representations of people, fragments of code who have been programmed to support your journey and enrich your experience. Their motivations are flimsy, made up, only revolve around helping you achieve your own goals. In real life, lots of guys seem to think women are NPCs. Women sometimes seem to believe it of themselves—too often, they are people who have grown up being taught at every turn that their story is to be a less important character in men's stories.

But men weren't taught that. They were taught that they are the hero. The protagonist. The central character.

---

24   Virginia Woolf, *A Room of One's Own* (London: Hogarth, 1929).

The one. The boy who lived. The son who could bring balance to the force.

You can never be the villain in someone else's story if you are always the hero in your own. When they say truth is stranger than fiction, what they mean is that there are limits to our collective imagination. Even now, in the overdigitized death throes of the disaster called late capitalism, so many men still can't imagine women being anything other than holes to fuck.

~

A few months after Valentine's Day, in the spring, Melissa was single, and I sprang my feelings on her in the midst of an MSN conversation about who I could see myself dating.

"Only two people," I told her. "You and Allie."

Those six words were a perfect encapsulation of all the reasons I wasn't much of a catch; casually admitting my feelings for her over IM chat, in the same breath as the ones I had for another girl, as if that wouldn't somehow ruin it, had she actually had feelings for me.

Perhaps it was an unconscious admission on my part that I knew I didn't have a chance in hell. I wasn't telling her the way you tell your love interest you have a crush on them; I was telling her the way you tell a friend about someone else you're crushing on. I had split her into two Melissas—friend Melissa and crush Melissa. I confided my feelings for crush Melissa in friend Melissa because the alternative seemed impossible.

Immediately, she laughed off the idea. "Do you have any idea what kind of a mess we'd make?"

I sat there at my desk for a few more minutes and let her tell me why my dream was a bad idea. When she was done, I grudgingly agreed with her. If I pretended I wasn't hurt, I wouldn't actually feel the hurt, like how cartoon characters can keep walking on air as long as they don't look down.

After that conversation, I still hung on. I'd like to say that I did it because I was a forward-thinking young man, but I wasn't. I was a boy drowning in an ocean of loneliness and self-doubt, opting for what seemed like the budget life raft because the deluxe model was no longer an option.

I didn't want Melissa to want to be my friend. I wanted to hold her, to kiss her, to sleep with her. But I was young, and lost, and lonely. I was also lucky, in a way. Lots of guys, in my position, would have left then and never looked back. But I was absolutely not proud enough to turn down her friendship just because she didn't want to hold my hand.

So I hung on. Hung on as Melissa started dating the 23-year-old banker who'd bought her candy hearts. Hung on as she convinced me to go to the same local college as her. Hung on when we started school in the fall, in sister programs, taking many of our classes together, those Monday mornings when our tracksuit-wearing professor yelled at us until our essays weren't bad anymore.

Somehow, that fall I ended up in a relationship with someone Melissa and I had been hanging out with, a girl in her program named Marie who asked me on one of those is-it-or-isn't-it dates.

Marie ended up breaking up with me after just five weeks, though, and I cried for the first time in years, lying alone in my parents' bed, thinking of how I'd never get to hold her again.

A year later, with my grades flagging and the reality that most university programs were beyond my grasp, Melissa convinced me to apply to a local university's creative writing program. I dropped a hastily concocted portfolio into a wooden box in a building downtown, certain that I was slipping it into the wrong box, certain that I would never hear back, certain that I would soon come up hard against a whole lot of dead ends.

I ended up getting in, though. And, as I'll explore later on in Chapter 12, listening to her advice was often one of the best decisions I ever made.

~

Most men have been taught that women are impossible to understand, or not even worth trying to, and I don't entirely blame them for buying into it.

I didn't know how many tampons a woman might go through in a year until college, when I guessed 12 and a female friend lovingly corrected me. I'd been close friends with more women than men for as long as I could remember, and I was still totally clueless about the menstrual experience.

Most men are missing the kinds of things you learn about women only when you are friends with them—only when you treat them as people, as equals, as peers, not as problems to be solved, rulers to be dethroned, locks to slide keys into and open.

~

After my first couple years of college, I'd shed my virginity and my religion, and joined the student paper, which offered me an avenue to express myself, to grow as a person. I started finding myself in relationships, or casually making out with people at concerts or on benches. Later, after I landed my job at AskMen, I'd even be called a "ladies' man."

Somehow, I had become a person with self-confidence, who women liked spending time with. And I knew, in my heart of hearts, I owed it to my friendship with Melissa, and the way that friendship had led, directly and indirectly, to other friendships with other women. By now, the overwhelming majority of my close friendships were with women, and it meant that I knew how to talk to women and that women felt comfortable around me.

The reaction most guys have to the word "friendzone" is a subtle, almost imperceptible shudder. Some have escaped it, some are struggling with it; some are so deep in it they can't perceive its existence. But the truth is, being friends with women is perhaps the best thing a man can do for himself. I don't mean friends as in quietly waiting for her to become single so you can pounce. I mean the same friendship you have with your male friends: you like spending time together, and that's all there is to it.

~

Feminist theorist Marilyn Frye, in her 1983 book, *The Politics of Reality*, advances a fascinating vision of how straight men conduct their lives:

> To say that straight men are heterosexual is only to say that they engage in sex ... exclusively with ... women. All or almost all of that which pertains to love, most straight men reserve exclusively for other men. The people whom they admire, respect, adore, revere, honor, whom they imitate, idolize, and form profound attachments to, whom they are willing to teach and from whom they are willing to learn, and whose respect, admiration, recognition, honor, reverence and love they desire ... those are, overwhelmingly, other men. In their relations with women, what passes for respect is kindness, generosity or paternalism; what passes for honor is removal to the pedestal. From women they want devotion, service and sex.[25]

Though the essay is a revision of a talk given in 1981, it rings alarmingly true today, more than four decades later.

---

25   Marilyn Frye, *The Politics of Reality: Essays in Feminist Theory* (Trumansburg, NY: Crossing Press, 1983).

Outside of strictly sexual or familial contexts, so many straight men do not love women, do not cherish them the way they cherish their male friends.

Even being close to a woman is seen as unmasculine. One of the boys in Orenstein's book says that having a girlfriend is "gay"—a beautiful contradiction that's echoed in one of my favourite quotes from the TV show *30 Rock*. "Wanting to be with a woman? How gay is that?" asks Will Arnett, as the impossibly gay Devon Banks, trash-talking Alec Baldwin's impossibly straight Jack Donaghy. "You *win* sex against a man, that's as straight as it gets."

And it makes sense, on some level. Growing up, boys are fed stories of how different they are from women, that the difference is inherent rather than malleable. And it's true that it's not always easy being friends with someone you see as deeply unlike yourself, especially if there's a chance of physical or romantic attraction. You might have some false starts along the way. You might find yourself developing feelings, or realize they are developing feelings for you. These things happen.

You'll probably over-rely on female friends for emotional support. You'll have to work at being a good friend; work at being kind and thoughtful in a way that you may not have to be with your male friends. That's work. It's not the easy route.

But what also happens when you're friends with women is you come to understand them. You come to appreciate their humanity in a way that men who aren't friends with women tend not to. You see them as real people, as whole humans, with complex inner lives, with motivations, with hypocrisies, with inner goodness. You see that they're worth forgiving when they hurt others, that they're worth defending when others hurt them.

It's a strange thing, because our culture tells you not to do this. The phrase "best friend" for so many, first and foremost implies someone of the same gender, as does, it seems to me, just plain "friend."

And it's not something you can necessarily manufacture. Friendship can be a tricky beast, and one that can be ruined with a wrong word or two, a hug held too long, a month too many of radio silence. You can ask someone if they'd like to be friends, but you can't guarantee that they'll say yes.

But if they do, stick with it. It comes slowly at first, but as time goes by, you become someone else, the way someone who exercises every day changes into someone new, someone fitter, with new muscles filling out their frame.

If you're lucky enough in this world to meet a genuinely good person who simply wants to be your friend, take that opportunity. Even if she's a woman—especially if she's a woman.

2

~~real men don't~~
wash the dishes

"The male urge to soak a pan until someone else washes it."

—@jacgorelick

You've been, I'm assuming, to parties before. Food and drink are consumed, people lose themselves to the drug of human interaction, new friendships are forged in the crucible of conversation, people may feel a powerful attraction to those around them. After a few hours, the place is a mess.

If you're a guy, you probably don't spend too much time thinking about that last part. If you're not, chances are you've spent a good amount of time cleaning up while the guys don't think about it.

If you've ever really paid attention to this—and, again, if you're a guy, you probably haven't—it's a jarring split. No one ever announces, "OK, time for all the women to clean up, and then men can stay where they are and have important conversations," and yet functionally that dynamic reproduces itself over and over in parties and social gatherings of all stripes all across the world.

Of course, this isn't the case in every culture, and certainly it's rarely explicitly gendered. Some women may stay and chat with the boys, and maybe a guy or two will grab some plates or some bottles in a show of well-meaning solidarity. But particularly in North America, the people doing the most cleaning will, without fail, be women, and the people doing the least will, without fail, be men. In fact, I'd wager that you're more likely to see a female guest cleaning up as a party winds down than a male host.

There's no great mystery there—women are socialized to attend to the domestic space, and men are not. And even if you're on board with the weirdness of the divide, you have to admit that it's not high on the list of priorities when it comes to fixing societal problems. You'd have to attend a party damn near every day for the accumulated differences to feel super important. How much time and effort goes into tidying up after a house party, anyway?

The only problem is, the party isn't where it ends—it's where it begins.

~

By now, a good chunk of the population is familiar with the name Jordan B. Peterson, something you can't say about the average professor emeritus, clinical psychologist or amateur Kermit the Frog impersonator.

Peterson made a name for himself during the second half of the 2010s largely through his lectures being uploaded to YouTube, and quickly became a favourite of the online right, thanks in large part to his attacks on "cultural Marxism" and his anti-trans views, but also thanks to the broad palatability of his core messaging, which was largely aimed at disaffected men and boys, and which bore language that resonated with them in a way that no one else's seemed to.

In short, he was filling a gap in the market, and he rose to unexpected prominence, quickly gaining a reputation as a leading intellectual figure despite the porousness of a lot of his thinking. (Google the diagrams from his debut book, *Maps of Meaning*, if you want to see what it looks like when someone takes themselves a bit too seriously.) This all culminated in his 2018 book, *12 Rules for Life: An Antidote to Chaos*, which became an international best-seller despite generally negative reviews from the critics.

The titular 12 rules included things like "Stand up straight with your shoulders back," "Treat yourself like you are someone you are responsible for helping," "Make friends with people who want the best for you," and "Compare yourself to who you were yesterday, not to who someone else is today."[26] On the surface, all of those are technically bits of good advice, and if you've taken even a little peek at the table of contents in this book, you know that the adage about not judging a book by its cover can also apply to chapter headings.

But one of Peterson's chapters really took off when it comes to our common cultural lexicon, and that's the

---

26   Jordan B. Peterson, *12 Rules for Life: An Antidote to Chaos* (Toronto: Random House, 2018).

chapter on cleaning your room—or, as he puts it, "Set your house in perfect order before you criticize the world."[27]

If you're familiar with the Bible, you might recognize a certain religious logic there—from Matthew 7:3–5, "Why do you look at the speck of sawdust in your brother's eye and pay no attention to the plank in your own eye? How can you say to your brother, 'Let me take the speck out of your eye,' when all the time there is a plank in your own eye? You hypocrite, first take the plank out of your own eye, and then you will see clearly to remove the speck from your brother's eye." It's an odd bit of metaphor that combines carpentry with ophthalmology, but the core idea still holds a lot of cultural weight to this day—which is unfortunate, in a way.

I disagree a lot more fervently with many other parts of the Bible (injunctions against tattoos, gay sex and menstruating women, off the top of my head, to say nothing of the holy war and slavery parts), than with that passage from Matthew. And I disagree a lot more fervently with many other things Peterson has said (his bigotry against trans people, his endorsement of an all-beef diet and his implication that putting a curvy woman on a magazine cover is "authoritarian tolerance," among others) than with the aforementioned chapter title. It simply strikes me as awfully shortsighted to ban any and all criticism unless the critic is themselves faultless.

You don't need to be an accomplished filmmaker to recognize that a terrible movie is bad; you don't need to

---

27   Peterson.

be a professional athlete to freak out when your favourite team is struggling, and you definitely shouldn't have to be perfect in order to call out cruelty and wrongdoing on the part of others.

It may not feel great to be on the receiving end of criticism, and in that space of hurt we may perform a quick scan of our opponents for weak spots we can turn against them, but that doesn't mean their critique isn't valid. It's an ad hominem attack, a logical fallacy that's often compelling enough to shut down an argument but that doesn't actually hold water.

In short, I don't think it's important to have your house in perfect order before you criticize the world at large. But I take issue with Peterson's thinking in another, more important way—one that strikes at the core of why his advice is both problematic and particularly appealing for young men.

~

As I write this, both my bedroom and kitchen are in sorry states.

Nine books—ten if you count the one propping up my fan—a dirty plate, two empty water bottles, a pair of jean shorts, an eraser, a pair of headphones, two bookmarks, a pair of socks, a backpack, a half-full travel-pack of Kleenex and a crumpled-up Kleenex dot the floor around my bed.

In the kitchen, a frying pan still crusty with scrambled egg residue sits on the stove; the counter features a stack of dirty plates and bowls, two empty glasses (one full of unwashed cutlery) and an assortment of dirty kitchen utensils lies in the sink.

In short, my personal space is in a bit of disarray, and by now you may be wondering as to my qualifications to tell anyone the importance of cleaning anything, whether it's your bedroom, your dishes or any other part of the home. (You see now why I just spent a few hundred words arguing for the importance of listening to hypocrites.)

Peterson's "clean your room" rhetoric earned him both accolades and acolytes, but it also earned him detractors for its seeming simplicity. *This is your king*, people seemed to be saying, *this is who you're all going crazy about? Your mom was asking you to clean your room up all those years and it takes a skinny, suit-wearing Canadian with a Ph.D. to make it stick?*

If you watch Peterson talk about this principle, he tries his best to gussy it up with academic language, but the long and short of it is that cleaning the space around you, the things you're in control of, will make you feel better.

And that may or may not be true. For me, cleaning my space is a mixed bag at best. Sometimes it makes me feel better, but usually the messiness I'm addressing is a sign that other things in my life are going badly rather than it being a bad thing in and of itself. When I get into a better headspace, I can clean my room, wash my dishes and tidy the rest of my apartment without too much difficulty.

The real issue I take with Peterson's approach is that, while he is taking the shocking decision to incite modern men to take up "women's work," he's doing it in a very prototypically male way. He's encouraging you to take care of your own house, rather than concern yourself with the world at large.

And while exhorting men to pick up a brush and dustpan, do some laundry and run a rag across their desktop might have the slightest tinge of the radical, telling men their self-improvement comes from controlling things that belong to them is about as avant-garde as a stone-age axe.

It's like the famous saying about the forest's falling trees. If a man cleans his bedroom till it sparkles but is still an asshole to others, does anybody give a damn?

That's why this chapter opened at the party you're invited to, not in your own kitchen. I don't really give a damn if you do your own dishes, and neither will anybody else who's not your roommate. My question is: when was the last time you did someone else's?

The crux of modern masculinity and what separates men from other genders is that men don't go out of their way to do the dirty work when others will do it for them. They won't fight to do the dishes at the party when all the women just congregated in the kitchen to do it first.

And as small as that moment may feel, it's emblematic of so many more situations where men make the exact same choice—to let someone else, most often a woman, handle things that need to be done—while they do something that they *want* to do.

This isn't just the guy leaning back and talking sports with the other guys at the dinner table as their wives, mothers, sisters, girlfriends and friends clean up, it's the gamer staying up to all hours playing *Call of Duty* and then not having any time to nicely wrap his girlfriend's present.

It's the dad who lets his wife handle all the kids' stuff and then is totally clueless about details like the dentist's phone number or what to make for lunch when Mom is laid up sick for a few days. It's the senior citizen who's been utterly alone in his room for a year since his wife died because she was the one who ran their whole social life.

Men letting women do "women's work" while they goof off is so ingrained in the fabric of our lives that most people don't even notice it anymore. Men are trained practically from birth to treat the women in their lives as some sort of weird secretary/nanny/personal assistant combo, and when they're deprived of access to that free labour, things can come crashing down in a hurry.

But the thrust of my argument isn't the Petersonian tack that it's better for you to familiarize yourself with how things work for your own sake—it's that it's better for the women in your life.

~

How much was your mom paid for raising you?

I'm kidding, of course. Moms don't get paid to raise their own kids. And yet the genuine work they put in at home is something that's worth money on the open market—because nannies, cleaners, cooks and all manner of people get paid to do that labour by rich families every single day.

In fact, a September 2015 McKinsey report suggested that the unpaid domestic work women do is worth nearly $10 trillion, or roughly an eighth of the existing global

GDP.[28] That's right—the women who stay home and take care of their kids aren't just stay-at-home moms, they're unpaid labourers who make up a significant, overlooked chunk of the economy, the grease that keeps the wheels running in more ways than people realize, since millions and millions of men benefit from the unpaid labour of female partners and/or family members.

You could (and maybe you should) argue that it's reductive and crass to put the beautiful bond between a mother and her child into financial terms. But not all the labour is lovey-dovey.

Ask a mom whether she'd like to get paid for changing a diaper instead of doing it for free, and I have a feeling you'd get some takers. Ask a mom cleaning up her fifth juice spill of the week whether she'd be up for a little monetary bonus for her time and effort and sure, some would pooh-pooh the idea away—but many wouldn't.

Perhaps the clearest articulation of the fact that parenting is labour is how little men do. According to 2016 Pew Research Center data, American fathers engage in only eight hours a week of childcare on average, compared to 14 for mothers.[29] That's a significant split, considering women now work nearly as long hours as men.[30]

---

28   McKinsey Global Institute, *How Advancing Women's Equality Can Add $12 Trillion to Global Growth*, September 1, 2015, https://www .mckinsey.com/featured-insights/employment-and-growth/how -advancing-womens-equality-can-add-12-trillion-to-global-growth.
29   Gretchen Livingston and Kim Parker, "8 Facts About American Dads," Pew Research Center, June 12, 2019, https:// www.pewresearch.org/fact-tank/2019/06/12/fathers-day-facts/.
30   Livingston and Parker.

Feminist, modern-masculinity dads may pay lip service to how important it is to contribute at home, and how precious the time they spend with their kids is, but that's not reflected in the data on heterosexual couples. These two sentences from a 2018 *Atlantic* article about the relationship between dish-washing and marital issues feel particularly damning: "Women who wash the vast majority of the dishes themselves report more relationship conflict, less relationship satisfaction, and even worse sex, than women with partners who help. Women are happier about sharing dishwashing duties than they are about sharing any other household task."[31]

Yes, it's possible to be so unengaged with the work of cooking, cleaning and tidying that someone divorces you for it—men can be so lazy it ruins their lives. And those whose marriages don't break up over labour division are often no more equitable than their newly single counterparts—they're just in marriages with more forgiving partners.

That's not just anecdotal. In a 2017 Stanford study, women asked for over two-thirds of the divorces, and male partners' perceived failures in the realm of housework were seen to be a significant contributor.[32] It seems like men's genuine inability to force themselves to do this work is slowly sapping their love life of its magic.

And it does make sense. If you've ever been assigned to work in a group on a school project, you know there's

31   Caroline Kitchener, "Doing Dishes Is the Worst," *The Atlantic*, April 3, 2018, https://www.theatlantic.com/family/archive/2018/04/doing-dishes-is-the-worst/557087/.
32   Michael J. Rosenfeld, "Who Wants the Breakup? Gender and Breakup in Heterosexual Couples," 2017, https://web.stanford.edu/~mrosenfe/Rosenfeld_gender_of_breakup.pdf.

no love lost for the least helpful member of the group. If one of your coworkers keeps phoning it in, showing up late and half-assing his work, that can get to you. If you've ever been on a sports team and watched one of your teammates just dogging it, you know that not putting in your fair share of work can be detrimental to a sense of team unity.

Yet too often, guys don't bring that mentality to their relationships. Because they were told early on that it didn't matter. Their mothers cooked and cleaned for them, folded their laundry, and they watched their dads get away with not doing much either. So it's not a surprise that they're not bringing the A-game to household chores.

~

What was I saying about hypocrisy earlier?

My own issues with cleaning and chores go back about as far as I can remember. I have pretty clear memories of balking at being asked to tidy things, wash things or sweep things around the home from probably about the age of 10 or 11.

Though my parents expected me to do chores as much as my sister, we were both born into a world that expected girls to do more chores than boys over the course of their lives.

It's impossible to avoid this logic. It's in our movies, our books and our pornography (ever seen a man in a French maid outfit?). I don't just mean that in narrative terms, either—I mean it's braided into the very fabric of our culture. We expect men to create things, and women to help pave the way for them.

As the Swedish writer Katrine Marçal explores in her 2012 book, *Who Cooked Adam Smith's Dinner?*, the man responsible for so much of the history of economic thought benefitted from this kind of freedom in ways that escaped his own notice.[33] Writing about Marçal's work in his 2020 essay collection, *Shit Is Fucked Up and Bullshit*, Malcolm Harris juxtaposes Smith's words in *The Wealth of Nations* ("It is not from the benevolence of the butcher, the brewer, or the baker that we expect our dinner, but from their regard to their own interest.") with this telling detail: "Smith, the originator of what we now call economics, may have imagined a table set with self-interest-filled plates, but he didn't cook his own meals, nor did he pay anyone to do it for him. He didn't go from one devotee's house to another like an ancient Greek, and he didn't sit at a patron's table like a court painter. Instead, he had his mommy do it."[34]

In Joanna Zylinska's 2018 book, *The End of Man*, she, too, encounters a primary text about a well-known male genius—the scientist Stephen Hawking—in Hélène Mialet's 2012 book, *Hawking Incorporated*:

> What is most interesting about Mialet's book is that she treats "Hawking" not as unique due to having to rely on an external network of collaborators and instruments because of his disability but rather as

---

33 Katrine Marçal, *Who Cooked Adam Smith's Dinner?: A Story of Women and Economics* (London: Portobello Books, 2015).
34 Malcolm Harris, *Shit Is Fucked Up and Bullshit: History Since the End of History* (Brooklyn, NY: Melville House, 2020).

just an extreme-case scenario of many great men of science and history who have had to function as part of the intricate network of humans (wives, secretaries, cleaners, research assistants) and non-humans (technologies of writing, computational machines, as well as lab, office, and home infrastructures) in order to accomplish things. Yet these enmeshed networks have had to remain obscured for the myth of the singular genius to be developed and sustained.[35]

What would a world where Adam Smith's mother and Stephen Hawking's female assistants got more credit look like? How many of your favourite movie directors spent their youths sweating away at home cleaning things? What would your favourite musicians have sounded like if they'd been asked to do chores instead of practising? Of course, it is possible to do both—but how many young women are afforded the right to pursue their genius without ever lifting a finger around the home? As Woolf explored in *A Room of One's Own*, without the necessary material preconditions for success, not even special talents can flower. Our culture simply has a habit of granting those preconditions much more easily to some than to others, whether it's family money passed down from white parents to white children or the freedom to explore, dream and experiment granted to boys and not girls.

---

35 Hélène Mialet, *Hawking Incorporated: Stephen Hawking and the Anthropology of the Knowing Subject* (Chicago: University of Chicago Press, 2012).

Between the time I wrote the first draft of this chapter and when I finalized the edits on it, my circumstances changed in several ways, but one of them, in fact, was dish-related. Today, I'm living in an apartment with a dishwasher. It's the first time I've lived with one since I was still living with my parents a decade and a half ago, and it's a luxury most of my peers do not currently have. It changes, in ways big and small, the simple question of doing the dishes, which can feel incredibly insignificant until the precise moment when it's your turn to do them.

No longer do the plates pile up in the sink. Now, the sheer monotony and time-consuming quality of dish-washing is replaced with the much shorter, less messy process of loading and unloading and the occasional pressing of some buttons and popping in a dish pod. My partner and I agreed early on in our cohabitation that I would be in charge of unloading the dishwasher. That felt like an opportunity for me to live my politics, as it were. But as the dishwasher took the bulk of the work off my hands, I somehow found myself backsliding, wanting to wash dishes even less now that I felt I didn't have to. So I still found myself avoiding small instances of washing, say, for the few kitchen items that we don't put in the dishwasher—in particular, a large non-stick pan.

I was reminded of this by a viral tweet I saw, which I used as an epigraph for this chapter: "The male urge to soak a pan until someone else washes it." The tens of thousands of likes those 12 words had gotten, despite the fact that they're not even a complete sentence, reminded me that this remains a gendered issue, and a widespread one, one that people can instantly recognize, one men will try to justify when really the reason is: "I wasn't socialized to do this work, so I will try to put it off as long as possible until someone else gets sick of it not having been done yet and just does it." Letting someone else fix it—a dishwasher, a roommate, a partner, a parent or the magical properties of water and time to soften food remnants off a piece of cookware—is seen as a preferable solution to simply rolling up your sleeves and handling it like a man.

So let's go over what handling it like a man actually looks like: you do not have the right to women's unpaid labour. Some men may continue to kick back and watch the women in their lives cook, clean and organize, but if you want to be a good man, you'll need to start doing your part.

Whether you clean your room or not is up to you—but what about your shared spaces? Are you vacuuming at home? Do you ever tidy up the car? Are you washing your dishes in the office sink or are you letting them pile up and hoping one of your female coworkers will get sick of waiting and do them for you?

Hell, even sending an email to everyone asking them to clean up is work, and it's exhausting to have to write that kind of message, finding the exact right tone that's partly funny and partly insistent without ever sounding like you're nagging or joyless.

In a just world, the cleaning duties are not split down gender lines even a little bit. In a just world, we afford kids the room to grow as people and to take care of the home in equal proportion. In a just world, there are so many female geniuses whose path to greatness was paved by their brothers or male partners taking care of all the housework while they perfected their craft.

We don't live in that kind of world, not yet. But the path there begins with men choosing to get up from the table after a delicious meal and plunge their hands into some soapy water while the women sit around chatting.

And depending on how used to doing dishes you are, you might do a bad job. You might not be as familiar with how to wash things as the women in the dining room. You might need to ask people which towel to use, where things go once they're dried and so forth. But the path to genuine equality passes through people like you choosing awkward moments over the familiar comfort of letting someone else do the work while you kick back.

These are little things, but like freshly washed plates stacked in a drying rack, they add up.

3

~~tough guys don't~~
listen to pop music

"Misogyny comes naturally to a young man in his late teens; it is a function of the powerful homosocial impulses that flower along Fraternity Row. . . . [Because] I was bright and a would-be artiste, my own misogyny wore a beret, as it were, and quoted Nietzsche. But it was just . . . garden-variety late-teenage, homosocial misogyny as practiced by young men all over the world. . . . It was a phase, a plankton bloom in the brain, a developmental stage, albeit one that found ample reinforcement, if not glorification, in culture both popular and highbrow, in the Rolling Stones's 'Stupid Girl' and Woody Allen's best movies, in Jorge Luis Borges, in William Shakespeare."

—Michael Chabon, *Manhood for Amateurs*

Like many people, my introduction to music was through what my father listened to. When I was growing up, around the turn of the 21st century, he had a phenomenal vinyl collection—literally many hundreds of records—and a ton of CDs too, and he was deeply passionate about music in a way that my mother wasn't. She would listen to beautiful classical music on the radio during the day while he was at work, but I connected much more intensely with what my dad played when he was home—the Beatles and the Beach Boys, Motown and Chuck Berry, the Velvet Underground and the Stooges, and, perhaps most formatively, punk rock.

It's weird to say your dad got you into hardcore punk, in no small part because his listening to hardcore punk when he was my age was a rebellion against his parents and their generation. That's the true spirit of punk: a big "fuck you" to the people in charge. Bonding with said people over a mutual love of revolt sort of short-circuits the very concept of punk. But my dad never really grew out of the rebellious music of his youth, so bond over it we did: he got me into bands like the Ramones, the Sex Pistols, Minor Threat, Black Flag, Bad Brains, the Dead Kennedys and the Misfits, and bought me their band T-shirts to match my budding enthusiasm.

There was something I couldn't ignore about the power in these bands' short, angry songs, the way they were designed to be played loud, written by people whose feelings could only be expressed in a snarl. It jibed with my experience of the world, as it had for him when he was my age, that it was a fucked-up place where the wrong people ran the show and the right people were always getting screwed. It didn't hurt that, overwhelmingly, nearly to a one, the bands were made up of people who looked like I did: young, able-bodied white guys, skinny and pale and not especially conventionally attractive. I didn't notice the glaring absence of people of colour or women at the time. As a white kid, it just reinforced my sense that what you needed to be a punk wasn't a look, a marketing plan or even talent, necessarily. For me, it seemed very populist—music by and for normal people who weren't interested in mainstream success.

~

At that age, I probably would have struggled with this next question, but I want to ask it of you anyway: who's your favourite female artist?

It could be someone known for music, for film, for visual art. It could be someone working in literature, modern dance, stand-up comedy. It could be someone who was a renowned actor or director or scriptwriter, a composer or a violinist or a drummer. It could be someone who works with paint, or someone who works with pixels. It could be any of the above or something else entirely. But it has to be someone. Because . . . you do have a favourite female artist, don't you?

For far too many guys, the answer is no, or not really, and if you're patting yourself on the back right now for coming up with one or two or even three names pretty easily, flip the script for a second.

Who's your favourite male artist?

Suddenly you have a longer list, right? And whittling it down to just one got a bit trickier. Suddenly you're not choosing between an actress you used to have a crush on and a female novelist you read for a school assignment, you're laying out a favourite director or two, three writers in three different genres, a half-dozen visual artists, and deciding which of two members of a rock group you think contributed more to the band's success.

You're not alone in this situation, of course. We're in a world that's historically supported the careers of male artists over, instead of and to the exclusion of the careers of female artists. It's not even exclusively a male problem—lots of women have a far easier time naming their favourite male artists. But it is a problem, and it both stems from and contributes to rampant issues of sexism in contemporary society, even in situations as seemingly meaningless as a nine-year-old boy looking at a pop album cover and going, "Ew, that's for girls."

The end point of that kind of thinking is a point where people start to imagine huge swaths of art, whole genres, entire mediums, are only intended to be consumed by one gender. It's a mentality that gets you YouTube comments like "i may be a straight guy but i'm not even gonna lie this goes hard" on a Cardi B song.

You might as well say, "I may be poor but this goes hard" about *The Great Gatsby* or "I may be from the 21st century but this goes hard" about the famous cave paintings at Lascaux. One of the most valuable and powerful things about art—a significant part of what makes it worthwhile at all—is its ability to translate something meaningful about the human experience across all these made-up borders we erect, the way a ghost passes through walls. Art is the human spirit manifesting itself in the world; any attempts we make to segregate it are backwards and, I believe, ultimately futile.

If you look at the art that women create and can't see anything of yourself in it, can't see a mirror of any of your own experiences, can't empathize with any of the pain on display or smile at any of the joy, the problem isn't with the art, it's with your worldview. But like I said earlier, you're not alone in the situation. And it is something that can be remedied.

~

If you've ever had to whine and wheedle to get a girl you know to watch a classically dudely movie or TV show with you, you're familiar with how frustrating it feels to watch someone write off a work of art that you genuinely connected with without giving it a fair chance. Now extrapolate that feeling to, well, the vast majority of men, and add a healthy dose of "this is unimportant and dumb" on top of your heaping portion of "this isn't for me" and you begin to get an idea of what women are up against when it comes to convincing the men they care about to take female art seriously.

There's nothing wrong with watching *The Wire*. Or *Die Hard*. There's nothing wrong with listening to Eminem. Or Pink Floyd. Or Kanye West. The problem creeps in when that's all you watch and listen to: art created by men, about men, for men. (And, far too often, it's just not just all men—often it's specifically straight, white men.)

When you do this, you're shutting yourself off to the humanity of everyone who lies outside those narrow boundaries. You're setting yourself up to be permanently clueless to the whole spectrum of humanity, of life, of emotion.

And it's a tricky problem, because it's easy to miss. There's no alarm that goes off if you're only into dude-bro art. There's no test that you fail, no grade you're held back from, no certificate you're not awarded. You can skate through life never genuinely engaging with female art and no one will notice unless they're looking very closely. That's not entirely your fault: school curriculums are so packed with straight white men that they're squeezing out basically every other kind of human being's art. They're factories for producing people who haven't engaged with art by the full spectrum of humanity.

When was the last time you read a book by a gay Asian woman? By a disabled or non-binary person? By a Black immigrant? These aren't hypotheticals or gotchas. They're real people who are alive on the Earth right now, and their life experiences have something to teach you about what it means to be a person—if you're willing to listen. But so long as we keep privileging stories written by the same kind of people over and over, no matter how diverse a selection of straight white men you have, you still have only straight white men.

And that does impact how you see the world, who you recognize as being worthy of not just your respect, but your admiration. Genius is everywhere. It's not something that privileged people have a divine right to, but until you're prepared to see it and to look for it, you might never genuinely grapple with its existence.

That's not to say that simply adding a handful of books by famous female authors like Virginia Woolf, Sylvia Plath and Toni Morrison to the high school syllabus will produce a generation of well-adjusted, non-sexist people. Rather, it's to say that consuming the art of a certain group of people is a necessary part of recognizing the wholeness of the group's humanity. Until you afford every other type of person the same respect you do to the canonical straight white man you've been taught to worship, you will struggle to genuinely appreciate the humanity that everyone else has.

That may be doable when it comes to things like disability, race, sexuality and so forth, but men seem to have special trouble with art created by women. That's no surprise! If you've spent your whole life being told that feminine traits are bad and something to be avoided, that to be girlish is to be weak and to be manly is to be strong, why would you seek out the thoughts and experiences and creations of the people who represent all those bad and un-masculine traits? It's like wearing pink—associate something with the "bad" gender often enough, and it becomes de facto bad itself. You can hear in your head a childhood bully asking you why you're reading that faggy book for girls. Hell, you can almost hear them saying, "Why are you reading at all?"

But that bully is dead wrong, and substituting their logic for your own is a form of weakness far worse for you than reading a woman's thoughts, watching a chick flick, or dancing to a pop song with abandon. That bully doesn't have your best interests at heart—they're trying to grind you down to fit a model that they understand, and if you sand off the parts of you that are genuinely interested in engaging with the world in order to fit into a rigid, old-fashioned mould of what a person can be, you'll be smaller for it—and so will your world.

~

Though angry music was my foundation during my teens, over the years, I realized there was also a certain something I couldn't ignore in a vastly different kind of music. Pop music in the late '90s and early 2000s—as it is today— was largely feminine coded, advertised to female and queer listeners. It didn't feel like music I had access to; didn't feel like music it was cool for me to like. And yet there I was, around the age of 12, asking for a Backstreet Boys CD for Christmas, understanding something about the Max Martin–produced beats and what they did to my limbs that I couldn't articulate, or pestering my father to get me Cher's "Believe" single after hearing it at the local skating rink and falling in love with its haunting, Auto-Tuned refrains. In my teens I would occasionally find myself dancing, alone in my room, to a Justin Timberlake song, trying to make my body do the things his did in his videos. I would find myself memorizing the lyrics to an *NSYNC single.

It felt ironic—of course it was ironic. Wasn't I the punk kid who religiously listened to angry rap-rock on my way home from school? And yet I got such a little thrill from it. I had no way to square these impulses. I kept it up through university, "ironically" liking Taylor Swift's love songs, Lady Gaga's dance tracks. Over time, though, I had to reckon with the fact that these likes weren't ironic, if it was even possible to like something ironically. I genuinely liked something about these songs, female-coded as they were. They spoke to something in me, a sense of joy and wonder that would come out when I had enough drinks in me—especially at weddings—as dance.

Dance is a fascinating aspect of human expression when viewed through a gender lens, because it's something far too many men see as a bit effeminate, if not extremely so. Ballet classes are supposed to be for girls, while the boys go out for team sports, right? And yet the desire to move your body to the rhythm of a song is universal for humans. While dance is so complex that only a handful of non-human species, like parrots and elephants can properly manage it,[36] for us, it's innate. Babies start responding to music in dance-like ways well before they turn two.[37]

---

36   Robert Krulwich, "The List of Animals Who Can Truly, Really Dance Is Very Short. Who's on It?" NPR, April 1, 2014, https://www.npr.org/sections/krulwich/2014/04/01/297686709/the-list-of-animals-who-can-truly-really-dance-is-very-short-who-s-on-it.
37   Heather Gowen Walsh, "6 Moves That Show Off Your Toddler's Developing Gross Motor Skills," *Parents*, February 18, 2020, https://www.parents.com/toddlers-preschoolers/development/growth/6-moves-that-show-your-toddler-is-developing/.

Dance is a part of us; it has been for at least as long as recorded history, and probably much earlier, if prehistoric cave paintings in India are indeed representations of early dancing, as some have theorized. Only powerful social conditioning could possibly rob you of that urge. My first taste of dancing was in the world of punk—slam dancing, or moshing, isn't necessarily the first thing that comes to mind when you hear the word "dancing," but it's still dancing: an admission that the music you're hearing is too powerful to sit still, that your body has to get involved one way or another.

Still, in North American culture—particularly in white culture, it seems to me—too often the dance floor in any mixed-gender situation is overwhelmingly female, with guys lined up at the sides, watching. It's not just a question of not wanting to dance at all, but also one of fearing judgment for participating in something they're not comfortable enough with to be good at. So long as dance remains female-coded, many guys would rather sulk on the sidelines than enjoy themselves and lose themselves to the magic of the music. They aren't only missing out on the chance to dance with attractive people—they're missing out on an essential, beautiful aspect of being human: letting yourself be overcome by the beauty of art, being one with your body and the bodies of others. Dancing is as close as you come to an orgy without taking your clothes off, a celebration of life, a testament to the joy of being human.

~

In Chapter 1, when I discussed the effects of not seeing women's stories represented in the pop culture we consume, I only touched briefly on the reasons behind that. Of course, there are tons of factors at play, but perhaps none more important than the fact that women are so rarely the ones creating the art that we encounter. Not because they don't want to, but because they aren't given an equal chance to succeed.

Historically, the powers that be that run the industries behind art production have been men, and they've been all too happy to let male stories and perspectives dominate. Take a look at the percentages of men in almost every category there is in Hollywood and you'll get a sense of what I'm talking about. Across the board, women are in the minority in every sector of the industry, making up as little as 5% in some filmmaking job categories, with screenwriters and directors—in effect, the people in charge of the stories we're consuming—being 80 and 90% men, respectively, according to some recent data.[38] These men then go on to tell stories about men, unsurprisingly, and when those are the majority of the movies on offer in theatres and online, well, that's what people watch.

The music industry is more slanted towards men, particularly behind the scenes.[39] Publishing is a bit different—women make up a large majority of the industry,

38   Women and Hollywood, "Statistics," https://womenandhollywood.com/resources/statistics/.
39   Andrew Limbong, "Women Are Still Missing in the Music Industry, Especially Behind the Scenes," NPR, March 31, 2022, https://www.npr.org/2022/03/31/1089901763/women-music-industry.

and indeed, this book might not have been published were that not the case. Still, that's only fitting, perhaps, since men don't buy as many books as women,[40] and it may be in no small part due to the reality of lower wages in book publishing rather than anything progressive. In the visual art world, there are issues too. There's data to show, for instance, that paintings by women still sell for much less than their male counterparts', though the gap appears to be thinning.[41]

Some of this is down to historical inequity and the fact that female artists so often surrender vast chunks of time they could have spent creating to domestic responsibilities or raising children—which, as you may recall from Chapter 2, is time-consuming, unpaid labour. But some of it is down to men's unwillingness to allow for the existence of female artistic talent as a feature of a more widespread sexism. In his 2015 book, *The Utopia of Rules*, the late anthropologist David Graeber has an aside about the way unequal gender roles have a dimming effect on the mind, and the relationship of that incuriosity to art.

40   Brooke Auxier, Ariane Bucaille, Duncan Stewart and Kevin Westcott, "The Gender Gap in Reading: Boy Meets Book, Boy Loses Book, Boy Never Gets Book Back," Deloitte, December 1, 2021, https://www2.deloitte.com/us/en/insights/industry/technology/technology-media-and-telecom-predictions/2022/gender-gap-in-reading.html.
41   Taylor Whitten Brown, "Why Is Work by Female Artists Still Valued Less Than Work by Male Artists?" Artsy, March 8, 2019, https://www.artsy.net/article/artsy-editorial-work-female-artists-valued-work-male-artists.

Generations of women novelists . . . have documented . . . the constant efforts women end up
having to expend in managing, maintaining, and
adjusting the egos of oblivious and self-important
men, involving the continual work of imaginative
identification, or interpretive labor. . . .Women
[are] expected to continually imagine what one
situation or another would look like from a male
point of view. Men are almost never expected to
do the same for women. So deeply internalized
is this pattern of behavior that many men react to
any suggestion that they might do otherwise as
if it were itself an act of violence. A popular exercise among high school creative writing teachers in America, for example, is to ask students to
imagine they have been transformed, for a day,
into someone of the opposite sex, and describe
what that day might be like. The results, appar-
ently, are uncannily uniform. The girls all write
long and detailed essays that clearly show they
have spent a great deal of time thinking about the
subject. Usually, a good proportion of the boys
refuse to write the essay entirely. Those who do
make it clear they have not the slightest conception what being a teenage girl might be like, and
are outraged at the suggestion that they should
have to think about it.

This logic, Graeber goes on to note, applies also to other
power imbalances, like race and class, and, as is so often

the case, compounds when they're layered one on top of the other.[42]

In a 2019 essay for *MEL* magazine about men's role models—which establishes how commonly male artists are considered just that—writer Madeleine Holden also points out how rarely women are cited as such by guys: "[A]n unwillingness to identify with womanhood and femininity is a cornerstone of traditional masculinity, and the reverse isn't true. . . . This prohibition on identifying with womanhood means that men and boys tend to view women as *women*—i.e., the Other—first, and as a set of potentially admirable characteristics, values and actions second, if at all."[43]

Between this dual unwillingness—the unwillingness to imagine and the unwillingness to revere—men end up with a genuinely skewed perspective of women. As long as they see women as an alien other, a group deeply unlike themselves, people to be excluded, dominated, subjugated, the problem will persist.

~

As someone who's spent much of the past decade of my life trying to redress the steep gender imbalance in my artistic

42   David Graeber, *The Utopia of Rules: On Technology, Stupidity, and the Secret Joys of Bureaucracy* (Brooklyn, NY: Melville House, 2016).
43   Madeleine Holden, "Talking to Men About Their Female Role Models Is Still Like Pulling Teeth," *MEL*, https://melmagazine. com/en-us/story/talking-to-men-about-their-female-role-models-still-like-pulling-teeth.

consumption, it's tempting—and it would be easy—for me to list, here, a selection of my favourite female creators: authors and poets, musicians and singers, directors and actors, painters and sculptors, dancers and performers, even memers and posters. Voila! An all-in-one starter kit for female art that'll promise to turn you non-problematic.

But the last thing I want to do is send anyone down a path they're already primed to dislike, only for them to recoil and dismiss the advice that sent them there. I don't know what you're into; a prepackaged list, no matter how carefully it's put together, how many tastes it tries to account for, is not what you need to get started on a journey like this.

What you need is simple: an attitude shift. While there is often less of it, and it's less well known, it's not like female art is something that's been hidden away from young men, kept under lock and key. It's there in the store, at the museum, in the streaming service's app, right next to the art created by men, waiting for you to give it a shot. The trick is starting to see female creators as people to flock towards, artists with a different vision of the world that have something important to teach you, rather than something to shy away from.

Art made by, for, about women might not be as highly rated—as a for-instance, IMDb voters are overwhelmingly male, and seem to give lower scores to female-coded films. It might not be as critically acclaimed, either, because the gender skew for film critics isn't much better. But that doesn't mean it's not as good. It just means it's different, and it might present the viewer with a different set of assumptions, a different moral compass, world order, overall sense of feeling. And if all you're used to seeing (and respecting) is art that's made with men in mind, approaching female-coded art—whether it's made by women at all—might mean you have to perform some of David Graeber's interpretive labour, to imagine what it's like to be someone who's different from you.

But if you start looking into it, what you'll find is that, whatever kinds of art you're into, women are making it too. They may not be doing it as often, and might not be getting the same accolades for it, but they are engaging in every genre, medium and form of art there is. If you can't see them yet, you're not looking hard enough.

And, of course, you should start looking into genres that you don't yet count among your favourites. Hence the title of this chapter—listen to pop music. When I say that, I'm not arguing that all pop music is feminine, that all women make pop music, that all pop music is good, that songs made to make people dance are better than songs that don't or that all art that's female-coded is inherently worthwhile. Women make trashy schlock crap just like men do, and women make cringe-worthy art just like men do. When I say listen to pop music, what I mean is: not all good art was created by men, for men. Some of the angriest, scariest hardcore I've ever heard was played by women; some of the frilliest sonnets I've ever read were penned by men. In no small part because gender markers that may seem set in stone (like, say, who wears wigs, or heels, or makeup—even the colour pink) actually change significantly over time, gender is not a useful lens through which to categorize art or decide what to engage with.

If you're a guy who's always felt that art made by women was tainted by the stain of femininity, learning to genuinely engage with female creations is an uphill battle. But it's one that is worth the payoff. You'll have your mind expanded—you'll literally find yourself becoming a more interesting and complex person. And you might just find yourself getting more comfortable on the dance floor.

4

~~if you're a real man you never~~
cry in front of your friends

"I never had any friends later on like the ones I had
when I was twelve. Jesus, does anyone?"

—The Writer, *Stand by Me*

Who's your best guy friend? How well do you know
him?

I don't mean what his name is, how old he is, what he
looks like—details that anyone who's a bit observant could
easily put together. I don't even mean the kind of stuff that
most male friendships consists of—what is he into, who
does he have a crush on, is he a jock or a gamer or both
or neither, what kind of music does he listen to, which
celebs does he follow online, how seriously does he take
school, what does he want to do with his life.

I mean a level of deeper knowledge. If someone asked
you both a series of personal questions about him, how
closely do you think your answers would match? Would
you even be able to answer a series of personal questions
about him? What's his favourite season? What was his life

78

like before he met you? What does he think about a given social or political issue? Has he ever truly loved anyone? What's the hardest thing he's ever gone through? Does he hope to have kids one day? And if so, what kind of a dad would he be?

If you're not especially confident in the answers to any of those questions, you're not alone. For so many guys, friendship is a surface-level thing, a question of overlapping schedules, the proximity of neighbourliness, the coworker, the fellow student, the regular attendee at your place of worship. You play pickup ball together, hang out and smoke weed, go to shows, snipe each other in your favourite video game.

And there's nothing wrong with that mode of friendship. It's fun, low-key, undemanding. No life is the worse for the presence of low-key, undemanding connections. With friends like that, you don't have to put yourself out for the other guy in any intense or exhausting ways. You're not finding yourself drained from all the emotional labour you've been doing after a hangout.

The problem is when guys don't ever go beyond that stage to forge deeper bonds with their friends, like the ones women do with each other. There are various extant stereotypes about women being catty and willing to throw each other under the bus for male attention, but these are increasingly recognized to be dated stereotypes and sexist misunderstandings. Contemporary female friendship seems like one of the strongest bonds in modern society, and there are movements within feminism today to reassess the value of lifelong friendships with other women relative to all-too-often brief and unpleasant romantic relationships with men.

One of the things that female friendships benefit from the most is vulnerability. Being able to see someone else suffering, to suffer with them, is a bonding agent. That's true in very feminine contexts, like coming over after work for ice cream and shared crying about a breakup; it's also true in very masculine ways too, though.

There's a reason people cite the bonds of military personnel as being some of the most intense a human being can experience. If you don't suffer along with someone else, if you don't go out of your way for them, if you're not prepared to go to extremes to protect them, how can you ever develop an unbreakable connection?

But there are other ways to foster closeness than shared suffering, and one way is simply being vulnerable in front of someone else. It's scary, because when we're vulnerable we're easy to hurt. But that's what makes exposing something about yourself special. In that moment, you are giving someone else the power to be cruel. But in trusting that they won't, you're affirming that there's a respect between the two of you, a trust that neither will try to do the other wrong. It's in that rich, fertile ground where real friendships start to take root.

~

Crying is one of the most vulnerable things about being human. It's a moment where we give ourselves over to the universe, where our bodies, against or without regard for our wills, act on our behalf, betray our innermost selves to the world. Whether it's a full-blown sob replete with trembling chin and audible wailing, a tear or two or a simple wetness around the eyes that can't just be blinked away, crying is a humbling, draining moment that people often associate with their moments of greatest pain, regret and sorrow.

Some research suggests that testosterone may inhibit crying.[44] Between that and research that suggests some of it is impacted by tear-duct size,[45] if you're a cis guy, there's a decent chance that the fact that you cry less than cis women and girls is down to biological factors. Many people transitioning, for instance, as part of masculinizing hormone therapy, report feeling fewer emotions than they used to,[46] and people taking estrogen report having more mood swings.[47]

But no matter how much testosterone you may have, you, too, own a pair of functioning tear ducts. The reason you cry less often and less easily may begin with biology,

---

44   Lorna Collier, "Why We Cry," *Monitor on Psychology* 45, no. 2 (February 2014), https://www.apa.org/monitor/2014/02/cry.

45   Melissa Dahl, "Why Do Women Cry More Than Men?" *The Cut*, January 7, 2015, https://www.thecut.com/2015/01/why-do-women-cry-more-than-men.html.

46   Jayne Leonard, "What is T therapy, and when can a person start it?" *Medical News Today*, March 17, 2021, https://www.medicalnewstoday.com/articles/ftm-testosterone.

47   Ashley Lauren Rogers, "8 Things That Really Happen When Transgender People Start Hormone Therapy," *Cosmopolitan*, September 29, 2015, https://www.cosmopolitan.com/sex-love/news/a46391/things-that-really-happen-when-trans-people-start-hormone-therapy/.

but it doesn't end there. Culture is a big part of it too. We socialize boys to avoid showing sadness from an early age, and those lessons stick. Men don't cry because, as boys, they were taught not to—and they almost never spend any time correcting that.

As I noted in Chapter 1, all too often, men withhold genuine love and respect from women in favour of caring about, listening to and being in solidarity with other men. But as unfair as that gatekeeping of their esteem winds up being, it doesn't even produce especially strong bonds with their fellow men. Too often it's a shallow form of love, if it can be called love at all.

Love is a special emotion, a designation of a closeness that surpasses others in depth and breadth. But we've gotten so wound up, as a culture, by a fear around the idea of two men actually caring about each other that we've normalized pumping the brakes on genuine closeness. Far too many guys can hardly profess to care about each other—the most basic of human experiences—without having to throw a "no homo" into the mix. So many men today are afraid to express tenderness or vulnerability in their friendships with other men that they wind up having sham friendships, shadow connections based on surface-level closeness, friendships that can fall apart at the lightest touch.

Imagine what you'd do if your best guy friend started crying in front of you right now. Would you pat him on the back, wrap him in a bear hug, sit with him and listen? Or would you cringe at the sight and pretend you hadn't seen anything, make an excuse and leave as fast as possible?

As the writer Andrew Reiner puts it in his 2020 book, *Better Boys, Better Men,*

> It doesn't matter that recent studies have touted the myriad benefits of crying—from lower blood pressure to the physiological benefits that accompany stress and anxiety relief to a reflex that encourages greater selflessness and compassion. All of that flies out the window when many of us witness someone sobbing in public. It's true that some people react with compassion and empathy at this sight and attribute sincerity to the crier. . . . But many of us, especially in the US, react differently. Some wire trips in our amygdala, and we jump to puff-chested judgments about the crier. . . .

The reason for that, Reiner speculates, is important. It's because "deep down, the lens really isn't on others. We do this with most displays of vulnerability. This very human, yet unforgivable, state triggers such heightened animus in us because, in the perceived weakness that makes us squirm, we see the compromised person who scares us most: ourselves."[48]

Being able to sit with tears—yours or someone else's—may seem elementary, but it's an act of remarkable strength

---

48   Andrew Reiner, *Better Boys, Better Men: The New Masculinity That Creates Greater Courage and Emotional Resiliency* (San Francisco: HarperOne, 2020).

and of compassion. One most men aren't brave enough to attempt, let alone pull off.

~

As a kid, I never seemed to understand how friendship worked. I think I finally sorted it out around the age of 14, but until then, I had vanishingly few friends. My model seemed to be to make a single friend and then try to squeeze every last ounce of closeness out of them until they were sick of me. First there was Tyrone, and then Tadzeo, and then Agustin. In high school, around the time I was developing a wider social circle and making genuine friends with girls for the first time, my best friend was a tall guy I'll call Mark.

Reaching 6'5" as a teen, and continuing to grow another inch or two in the coming years, Mark was a real physical specimen. He was everything I wasn't—or so I felt at the time. Handsome, charming, self-confident, blond-haired, blue-eyed, an athlete, a musician, a strong student. The kind of kid I never would have become friends with if not for the fact that he showed up halfway through ninth grade and his locker was right next to mine.

We ended up having a surprising number of things in common, though. We had very similar senses of humour, and a penchant for silliness and wordplay. We both also loved angry music. And, by happenstance, we took the same bus route to school. It wasn't long before we were genuine friends, and for the next few years, the friendship bled outside the lines of just school—we exchanged long emails about politics, music and the world, watched hockey games and TV shows at his place, chatted online on a near-daily basis, and even briefly attempted to start a band together. Our shared experiences and passion for language started to take hold—at one point, during our last year of high school, another friend said our conversations were so full of references and shorthand, listening to us talk was like seeing people converse in a separate language.

It was friendship as I thought it ought to be—close, tight-knit, deep and meaningful, but not without its share of moments that saw us on the floor in front of the TV, wheezing with laughter over the ridiculousness of some dumb joke. But it never occurred to me to open up to him about what the friendship meant to me, to navigate the boundaries of what we were to each other with the kind of care I would spend the rest of my life investing in my romantic relationships. Friendship was something that just *was*—or it wasn't. It wasn't something you could, or should work on, wasn't something that needed to be protected from anything, the way jealous partners guard the sanctity of their relationships.

But just because something works for a long time in a way that feels so natural that it doesn't require that kind of care or maintenance doesn't mean it's invincible. Whether you articulate them or not, everyone has boundaries, and they're never more real than when they've been crossed. Mark had pushed up against mine on a handful of occasions. When we hung out in group settings, the closeness between us too often seemed to melt away, leaving me on the butt end of his jokes. But I could forgive those little heel turns. Mark only really ever crossed my boundaries once—but in the course of a single night, he undid five years of some of the closest friendship I'd had in my life until then.

It happened by a lakeside cabin in northern Ontario. Mark had spoken for years about his family's place up there, but it wasn't until the summer of 2007 that he finally invited me. We had tickets to see two bands we both loved play together in Toronto, and he pitched the idea of stopping at this cabin in the woods for a few nights before heading to the city for the show. I was elated. Then he told me that a mutual friend of ours, Cathryn, would be coming too. I was a little hurt that he wanted to bring someone else along, and privately I found Cathryn a bit annoying, but she was part of our friend group and she, too, liked the bands we were going to see.

When we got there, though, I started to realize something was up. Mark was barely interested in interacting with me—he and Cathryn seemed like they were the actual focus of the trip, and me the awkward interloper. After a stressful and charged first night that ended in strip poker, a naked trip to the sauna and skinny-dipping—three things I'd never done before—by the second night, I was feeling exhausted. It was clear they were attracted to each other, despite both being in relationships with other people, and their flirtations were painful to watch. I pretended I was feeling tired and went to bed early just to avoid them.

A few hours later, I was awoken by their voices as they came to bed—in the tent the three of us were sharing not far from the cabin, where Mark's brother and his family were staying. Annoyed by the giddiness in their voices, I pretended to sleep through their entrance. Then I heard strange noises and realized what was happening: they were kissing. It wasn't long before I heard Cathryn start to go down on Mark. I was facing away from them but couldn't believe what I was hearing. I wanted to move, to speak, to do something, but I found myself frozen. I was panic-stricken. Mark's girlfriend was a friend of mine, and one of Cathryn's closest pals. The sheer number of different ways this was inappropriate was staggering.

Before long, they decided to move their hookup out of the tent, probably fearing they'd wake me up, not realizing they already had. My mind raced. How could they do this to me and to their respective partners? The next morning, I confronted them about what I'd heard. They were crestfallen, and the rest of the trip—we still went to the concert as planned—was incredibly, cringe-worthily awkward. When I got home, something between me and Mark had changed.

I tried to grapple with his betrayal by shifting the blame onto Cathryn. I vowed never to talk to her again, and to this day I still haven't. I couldn't give up on my friendship with Mark so easily, but I also couldn't meaningfully confront him about what he'd done. I'd never told him how much the friendship meant to me, so how could I lambaste him for being flippant about it? I had never had any kind of sex before, had never even French kissed anyone, and had certainly never been naked around other teens. Now, my first experiences of genuine physical intimacy had happened without my consent and, literally, behind my back. The seeming ease with which Mark turned what was supposed to be a fun trip for the two of us into an excuse to cheat on his girlfriend within a few feet of me while he thought I was sleeping was jaw-dropping in its thoughtlessness. In order to square that hurt with the friend-love I felt for him, I had to push all the anger onto Cathryn. At the time, it felt like a very personal, private thing, but in that moment, I was just another in a long line of people to blame a woman for a man's actions. The personal, as they say, is political.

~

In early 2021, the Japanese government appointed a minister of loneliness, recognizing that frayed and fraying social ties were a genuine hazard after an increase in the suicide rate.[49] It's a recognition of a glaring fact that most of the rest of the world has yet to wake up to: that the number, breadth and depth of your friendships is not kids' stuff. These are matters of life and death.

The impact of friendlessness is well-established by now, and it's not pretty. It's more than just something that leads to suicide—it's a silent killer, affecting mental and physical health in myriad ways that can go completely unnoticed. And it's particularly deadly for men. While the

---

49   Katie Warren, "Japan Has Appointed a 'Minister of Loneliness' after Seeing Suicide Rates in the Country Increase for the First Time in 11 Years," Insider, February 22, 2021, https://www.insider.com/japan-minister-of-loneliness-suicides-rise-pandemic-2021-2.

conversation around the Japanese government's decision highlighted a sharp increase in women dying by suicide, the truth is that men still make up well over half of the total.

And, of course, the vulnerability of friendless men when no one's paying close attention is acute, because for friendless older men, people rarely are. Friendless older men have less to live for, fewer people checking in on their well-being, less mental stimulation. When they develop symptoms of physical illnesses, as aging people so often do, they're less likely to get them checked out, as I'll discuss in Chapter 6, and there are fewer people to encourage them to do otherwise.

This is a bleak picture, and it's a significant factor in the reality of men dying years younger than women. Without a robust social net, and unable or unwilling to make the effort to begin socializing in new ways, they simply slip through the cracks. Many men in middle age offload the emotional labour of maintaining relationships to female partners. Sending a holiday card to a relative? That's a wife thing. Planning to host a dinner? That's a wife thing. Showing up with food for a friend who's in mourning? That's a wife thing. But if the relationship ends—whether in death or divorce—what he's left with is no clear idea of how to be a social being.

In a 2015 article for The Good Men Project, writer Mark Greene ties the socialization that young boys receive around how they can and can't act in their friendships with other boys to the horrifying effects of what many are calling an "epidemic of loneliness": "Let's take a moment to connect the dots. Boys feel fierce love for their best friends → Add homophobia, the Man Box, etc. → Boys disassociate from loving best friends → Boys and men become emotionally isolated → Men enter the epidemic of loneliness → Men die."

"We now have a clear and direct through-line," he continues, "tying rampant homophobia and the Man Box to resulting grief, isolation, and early mortality in hetero-sexual men."[50]

Sonora Jha, too, addresses this in her book *How to Raise a Feminist Son*. In India, where she was born, it's commonplace for male friends to hold hands in public, a practice that isn't perceived as homoerotic or effeminate. It wasn't until she moved to America as an adult that the lack of male touch in Western society leapt out at her: "American homophobia denies same-sex affectionate physical contact to its heterosexual men."[51] Even hugging a friend goodbye can be seen as suspect by some guys.

In this climate, it's no surprise that the act of saying something as natural and heartfelt as "I love you" becomes fraught. As Rembert Browne notes in a 2016 online piece for *New York Magazine*, "I love you, man" often conceals a longer, richer statement, like "I love you, man [for reminding me how to be good]," or "I love you, man [for not disappearing on me when I fell off the grid for a year or so]." "It's what's

---

50 Mark Greene, "Why Do We Murder the Beautiful Friendships of Boys?" The Good Men Project, February 26, 2015, https://goodmenproject.com/featured-content/adult-male-lonliness-megasahd/.
51 Sonora Jha, *How to Raise a Feminist Son: A Memoir & Manifesto* (Seattle: Sasquatch Books, 2022).

implied after that loving declaration," Browne writes. "It doesn't have to be said; you can feel it."[52]

And sure—there's something beautiful, sometimes, in the way things can be unspoken between two people who are truly close. But it's also possible to mistake that unspoken quality as a value in and of itself, and to leave things unsaid not because they don't need to be said, but because they can't be. Saying "I love you" to a male friend is a vulnerable act; Ken Budd, in a 2021 piece for the *Washington Post*, writes that appending "words like 'buddy,' 'man' or 'dude' [is] a common guy trick to soften the emotional impact" of saying "I love you." But as Budd notes elsewhere in his piece, "It's counterintuitive: We think 'I love you' projects weakness, but it takes strength . . . to be emotionally open in a culture that dissuades it."[53]

In contemporary North American society, male friendship is a tenuous thing. It's a bush planted in unfertile ground, that rarely sees sunlight or water. When it dies, withering away as you'd expect, it passes unmourned. And the garden of your life is that much poorer for it. But it doesn't need to be this way.

~

52　Rembert Browne, "What We Mean When We Say 'I Love You, Man," *New York Magazine*, May 25, 2016, https://nymag. com/article/2016/05/what-we-mean-when-we-say-i-love-you-man. html.
53　Ken Budd, "Why Can't More Straight Men Say 'I Love You' to Each Other?" *Washington Post*, May 10, 2021, https:// www.washingtonpost.com/magazine/2021/05/10/why-cant-more-straight-men-say-i-love-you-each-other/.

Men keep their friends at arm's length for fear of accidentally getting too close—and being punished for it. But living your life by never being vulnerable in hopes that it means you'll never be hurt just means you'll never be genuinely close to anyone. So when I say cry in front of your friends, what I mean is open up spaces of closeness with them that include the possibility of vulnerability—real, raw emotional vulnerability. Talk to them about your real self and ask them to do the same in return.

I don't know what my friendship with Mark would have been like if I'd been capable of opening up to him about how hurt I was by his betrayal. I don't know that my being vulnerable about the rawness of that pain would have elicited an apology from him, would have mended the hole he'd ripped in the friendship. Maybe he would have simply scoffed at me, turned his back and walked away. It's not out of the question; that exact fear, more or less, is what keeps men from voicing these hurts to their friends in the first place.

But I also know that, however closely he hewed to traditional masculine ideals in some respects, in many others he seemed to rebuff them. And I do believe he valued my friendship in a genuine and meaningful way. So I'd like to believe he might have been willing to meet the vulnerability on my part with a response that would affirm the connection we had rather than belittling it. And that that might have kept us from growing apart when he left for college, and that we might still have been friends to this day.

But I couldn't open up to him about the pain he'd caused me, and I carried that pride more comfortably than I could the vulnerability. And lost someone who used to be a kind of brother to me because of it.

I tell you this because you, too, will lose your brothers if you don't face the fact that friendship without vulnerability is no friendship at all. Whether you ever actually cry in front of each other isn't the point—the point is that you have to be willing, on some level, to go to that most vulnerable of places with the people who mean something to you if you want their friendship to matter in the long run. Because if you keep everything surface-level, the first time things get complicated they'll move on. And your pride may not weigh all that much, but loneliness is an especially heavy burden to carry.

Lots of guys like to use the word "bud" to describe their friends. I think that's apt—male friendship, too often, is like a bud, in the sense that it's something that hasn't yet flowered, hasn't yet grown to its full potential. So maybe it's time to turn your buds into something more.

5

~~a real man would never~~
fake an orgasm

"Everyone always lies about sex. If you haven't lied about it, it isn't sex."

—Carrie Fisher, *The Guardian* advice column

There aren't a ton of proponents of the fake orgasm. Apart from industry insiders in porn, old-fashioned 1950s love advice columnists for women and people who, like Cypher in *The Matrix*, prefer being lied to, typically, people prefer real orgasms—gushy, spine-tingling, muscle-spasming realness.

And yet, fake orgasms persist—in relationships, in hookups, in various forms of sex work. Some studies suggest that as many as two-thirds of women who sleep with men have admitted to faking one.[54] They're an

---

54   Charlene L. Muehlenhard and Sheena K. Shippee, "Men's and Women's Reports of Pretending Orgasm," *The Journal of Sex Research* 47, no. 6 (2010): 552–567, https://doi.org/10.1080/00224490903171794.

incredibly common reality that likely won't be going anywhere fast.

It's also noteworthy that, like lipstick, pepper spray and the colour pink, fake orgasms are an overwhelmingly, if not inherently, gendered phenomenon. Ask your male friends about the last time they faked an orgasm and they'll laugh; ask your female friends about the last time they faked an orgasm and watch as they all try to remember the most recent specific instance, whether it was a decade ago or just this morning.

(Of course, you might argue, it's harder for men to fake orgasm—they ejaculate. And sure, for the overwhelming majority of cis guys, each orgasm is accompanied by a spurt of semen that would be incredibly complicated to fake convincingly. When it comes to women, you might say, they can fake an orgasm just by moaning at a specific pitch, or even just by saying, "Wow, you just made me cum so hard" afterwards. But sex is not porn—most of it doesn't take place in hyper well-lit rooms, and much of it involves condoms. A guy faking an orgasm in the dark while wearing a condom is another story entirely, and most people are not going to hunt down the used condom in the garbage can and carefully inspect it for evidence afterward.)

In any case, I'm not arguing that every woman has faked an orgasm, let alone multiple. Though there are assuredly women who have faked every single orgasm they've ever told a partner about, for starters, not every woman has even had sex. Second, for some women, real orgasms come so naturally as to make it more complicated to fake one than to simply have one. Third, some women just place more importance on keeping it real than anything else.

But for many women, there is the reality that at some point, it's more economical, logical, aesthetically pleasing and/or downright kind to pretend you just came than to admit you didn't—or to simply gesture in that direction with a few well-placed moans and hope the question doesn't come up explicitly. No one wants to say, "Did I cum? No . . . cause you kind of suck at pleasuring me," right afterwards, and even saying "Did I cum? No . . . I have a lot of trouble orgasming from sex" or "No . . . but it's fine, I rarely do anyway" isn't a lot of fun either. Straight men are notorious for taking an admission that a partner didn't cum as an affront, and then before you know it, the bedsheets are a battleground.

There are a few different things at play behind the façade of the fake orgasm. For starters, there's the fact that women are typically socialized to place the desires of others before their own. And if your partner's desire is to feel like a powerful and impressive lover—most straight men do, and most straight women know that—then it makes a lot of sense to have the look and feel and sound of an orgasm in your tool kit—just in case a real one doesn't appear to be forthcoming.

Second, and perhaps most importantly, there's the fact that real orgasms often aren't forthcoming for straight women, because, apart from medical or psychological conditions that impede a real orgasm's arrival, spoiler alert: so many straight men, maybe even the majority, are not good in bed.

Depending on how many women have spoken to you about their sexual experiences, that might sound ludicrous, or it might sound boringly obvious. But if you doubt it, dear reader, I can assure you that it's the case. Ask the women who sleep with them and you'll hear that at all ages, across race, class and creed lines, straight men are, in general, bad at sex.

This isn't an immutable fact, etched in stone; it's a reflection of the fact that so much of straight sex finds men acting out scripts, trying to hit a target in their own head, rather than being present in the moment, in touch with and knowledgeable about their partner's body.

They could be good lovers if they genuinely applied themselves to the task—being good in bed isn't especially complicated, despite what some people selling sex advice will tell you—but they'd rather be bad lovers, because being bad in a stereotypically masculine way (focus on penis size, jackhammer penetration, cumshot on face, always being in control) feels more right to them than being good in a stereotypically feminine way (lots of foreplay, performing oral, post-coital cuddling, paying attention to physical cues).

Here again, we come up against the double-bind of masculinity: men want to be good at sex, but not if it means compromising their masculinity. But being bad at sex doesn't feel very masculine either. So they lie to themselves and others, minimizing the presence of competing narratives to feel like they've got it all figured out, and women lie to them to make them feel better about it by faking their orgasms.

Sex is full of slippery contradictions like that, ones that trouble the simple narratives masculine ideology would love to impose. Oral sex is a great one. What's more masculine, giving oral sex or receiving it? The man giving oral sex is active, making his partner feel pleasure, while the man receiving it is passive, receiving an experience he has no control over. Does the manly man tongue-fuck or does he get sucked off?

Porn tries to solve this dilemma with face-fucking, reducing the mouth of someone giving head to a mere orifice rather than a complex set of body parts (tongue, throat, cheeks, even teeth) that can be made to work together in an expert choreography by a skilled dick-sucker.

It's a cheapening effect, the degradation of something nuanced and exciting to a raw cruelty. To fit a narrative, to paper over the truth, which is that sex is interplay and that as much pleasure can be wrought from giving up control as from having it.

When you can come to terms with this fact, which I'll explore more in Chapter 10, whole new worlds of sexual potential will open up to you. It's possible, albeit unlikely, that you can be good in bed without a genuine understanding of the value of being vulnerable in bed, but once you accept vulnerability, your path to being a sexually dynamic lover becomes broad, well-lit, and smooth. In short, it'll simplify your journey.

I don't mean that you should seek out a dominatrix, kneel over and accept a spanking. I don't mean you get your partner to tie you up and pour hot wax on your nipples. (Though if those sound arousing, by all means, try them.) What I mean is you invite the possibility of a new narrative into bed with you, one that's not focused on your domination, one that's not focused on your being a manly stud, but that's focused on learning about pleasure—yours and your partner's.

And that's where the fake orgasm comes in. No, faking an orgasm won't make you a good lover. No, I don't think anyone *should* fake an orgasm, necessarily. In a perfect world, everyone would cum easily and often and no one would have any hang-ups about sex.

But the mindset where you let your partner's pleasure take the fore to such a point that you're willing to do almost anything, even pretend you're cumming when you're not quite there yet, to help them cross the threshold—that's where being a good lover lies. Until you get to the point of genuinely putting your partner's pleasure before yours, you're going to struggle to blow anyone's mind, let alone your own.

~

Like many people, my early experiences of sex weren't especially noteworthy. The first time I tried penetration with a partner, it lasted about a minute before I came. (The biggest upshot of those early explorations was my then-girlfriend helping me discover that I had phimosis—a condition some uncircumcised people experience where the foreskin doesn't naturally retract as the penis becomes erect. Though in some cases phimosis requires surgery to correct, mine did not; I quickly busied myself with stretching the opening little by little until I could pull it back all the way.)

I was 19 then, and over the next couple years, I'd have sex another dozen times or so. Some of it was fun, some of it was awkward and unpleasant. I didn't start having regular sex, and thus good sex, until 21, the first time I was in a relationship that lasted longer than a year. It was sexually revelatory for me: we tried different positions, fucked in the shower, in the basement, on vacation, on the floor. We wrote each other erotica, we sexted, we 69ed.

I spent most of the next three-quarters of a decade jumping from long-term relationship to long-term relationship. I didn't like being single, and I had the good fortune to come across people I was interested in and who reciprocated that interest on a regular basis. Which meant that, by the time I, newly single, started engaging in "meaningless hookup sex" for the first time, in the months leading up to my 30th birthday, I had pretty much only had sexual experiences with long-term partners.

That's not the rarest experience out there, but it's certainly not the most common. I had somehow made it to the doorstep of my 30s with barely a whisper of experience with what the media termed "hookup culture." I'd been editing and publishing other people's writing about that very subject for years, so I felt like I had a pretty good idea of what it was and how it worked, but it was an alien culture to me in many real respects. I'd never really had to go through the very real weirdness of navigating the morning after with someone you've just slept with, the negotiations of sexual boundaries mid-coitus, the way a text message silence in the days afterward can become unbearably loud.

But what surprised me when I did start hooking up with women in earnest was how surprising my behaviour was to them. They didn't expect me to want to go down on them, didn't expect me to be good at it, didn't expect me to be excited to extend an oral sex session past just a handful of minutes. Without any explicit tutoring, without taking any courses, I was being treated by my partners as something special in bed. My dick is average size, my stamina nothing to write home about, my musculature that of someone who'd been to the gym only twice. I'd edited dozens of articles about sex, but these were all available for free online. I didn't have an unfair advantage. I wasn't some sex god, but because almost every guy these women had slept with before me hadn't been interested in their pleasure, it felt like I may as well have been one.

In fact, the one hookup that really mattered that summer was with someone I'd go on to have one of the most significant relationships of my life with. We met to get drinks together and after we'd had a few, she invited me back to her place. After some conversation on her couch, we started making out, and she suggested we shift things to the bedroom. When I tried to put on one of the condoms she had in her dresser drawer, panic set in. I couldn't open the wrapper. I kept tearing at different corners, my fingers getting sweaty, freaking out about ruining the moment. Between that anxiety and the litany of drinks I'd had, by the time I did get the wrapper open, my erection was gone.

It was the first time I'd ever really grappled with the issue of erectile dysfunction, and it was an annoying time for it to rear its head, since I already knew that I really liked this person. I apologized—and suggested I go down on her for a bit instead. After a little bit of that, I was hard again, and we tried again, but the next condom wrapper proved just as tricky, and eventually I gave up on penetration entirely. Going down on a gorgeous, funny woman seemed like a lot more fun than doing nothing, so it wasn't bad as a consolation prize. We probably spent close to an hour together, naked in bed, without even a minute of penetrative sex—but it was awesome.

The next morning, to my surprise, she asked me if I wanted to see her again that night, and a few weeks later, asked if she might come visit me in my hometown. Not long afterward, we started dating seriously. In a way, that whole relationship owes its existence to my willingness to go down on her rather than focus on my own pleasure the first time we hooked up. If I'd struggled forward, insisting on penetration either without a condom or vainly trying to shove a flaccid dick into her, if I'd insisted that she go down on me, it might have been such an unpleasant experience for her that none of our years of happiness together might have come to pass.

(And when she came to visit me a few weeks later, the erection issues had magically vanished. As I learned later while writing an article about the science behind erections, stress over not being able to open the unfamiliar condom packaging had activated my sympathetic nervous system, making sexual arousal an uphill battle. With my usual condom brand on hand, it was easy to stay in the relaxed headspace of the parasympathetic nervous system, where arousal can flourish.)

~

The hookup culture I mentioned earlier isn't some historical accident—it's a product of shifting socioeconomic factors over the past century. It's worth quoting the writer Hanna Rosin's breakdown of what happened, from her 2012 book, *The End of Men*, at length:

> A woman's sexuality has social value, and she trades it for other things she wants. In the old days the exchange was fairly obvious. Women traded sex for security, money, maybe even social and political influence. Because they had no other easy access to those things, it was imperative they keep the price of sex high so they had something to bargain with. Now women no longer need men for financial security and social influence. They can achieve those things by themselves. So they have no urgent incentive to keep the price of sex high. The result is that sex, by the terms of sexual economics, is cheap, bargain-basement cheap, and a lot of people can have it.

The upshot of that transformation hasn't been an explosion of sex—studies have shown repeatedly that for a long time now, contemporary young Americans are having noticeably less sex than the generations before them[55]—but that's not an indication that Rosin is wrong. (As she says, a lot of people *can* have it—"can" being the operative word.) Rather, it's a sign that more and more people are choosing not to pursue in-person sexual contact, given the option.

Some of that is likely down to cultural factors around digital technology: the rise of internet porn, the increasing atomization of our social lives leading to online interactions replacing IRL ones, and stuff like video calls and teledildonics supercharging the possibilities of long-distance sex. (And some of it, I'm coming to believe, is due to increasing levels of economic precarity meaning people are simply too stressed out to be horny.)

But some of it, too, is likely that for many women, sex with men is not as enticing as straight men have been led to imagine.

Faced with the prospect of being vulnerable around a guy who probably won't be able to (or even bother to try to) make them cum; might care little, if at all, for their sexual and reproductive health; might, intentionally or otherwise, subject them to traumatic experiences in the moment; and will likely act rudely in one of several different ways afterward, even horny straight women can

55   Kate Julian, "Why Are Young People Having So Little Sex?" *The Atlantic*, December 2018, https://www.theatlantic.com/magazine/archive/2018/12/the-sex-recession/573949/.

be forgiven for opting for porn-watching and toy-enhanced masturbation over hookups.

If you don't believe me, consider that there's even a term for what's going on here. It's called "the orgasm gap," and it's a reflection of what's shown up time and again in studies of people's sexual experiences: when people have heterosexual sex, women experience orgasms much less often than men do, to the tune of something like 20 or 30 percentage points lower.[56]

People for whom the current arrangement is comfortable might be happy to write this off—either as a biological fact that can't be changed, or as irrelevant, or both. But it's not an accident. As Peggy Orenstein puts it in *Boys & Sex*, citing work by researcher Lisa Wade, "Wade found that, whether consciously or not, boys signaled a partner's lack of value to them by denying her orgasm and the activities that would most likely produce it (though, at the same time, guys also overestimate women's orgasms in hookups by a third to a half, either out of ego, ignorance, or because the girl faked it)."

Ask yourself how crazy you'd be about rushing head-first into a sexual encounter if it looked like this: you were meeting up with someone who, statistically, was going to be bigger, stronger and more violent than you, who wasn't

---

56   D.A. Frederick, H.K. St. John, J.R. Garcia and E.A. Lloyd, "Differences in Orgasm Frequency Among Gay, Lesbian, Bisexual, and Heterosexual Men and Women in a U.S. National Sample," *Archives of Sexual Behavior* 47 (2018): 273–288, https://doi.org /10.1007/s10508-017-0939-z.

going to make you orgasm and who would focus almost entirely on their own pleasure.

No matter how hot this person is, it doesn't sound quite as fun, does it?

~

My experience with hookup culture the summer before I turned 30 was eye-opening for a few reasons, but the one that's most important for most young men is how easy it is to impress a woman in bed.

That's one of the sad truths about hetero hookup culture—to quote Orenstein in *Boys & Sex* again, "hookup culture aligns with the values of conventional masculinity: conquest over connection, sex as status-seeking, partners as disposable"[57]—but it is useful for guys with a willingness to apply themselves. Because of the sheer listlessness of the average guy in bed, you can easily distinguish yourself from the pack, and one of the best ways to do that is to focus on non-penetrative sex.

The phrase "non-penetrative sex" might sound like a contradiction in terms to some. For far too many people, sex is penis-in-vagina penetration. But the truth is, even if you include penis-in-anus penetration, you're still leaving out a whole lot of fun for a whole lot of people. At its core, sex is fluid. What it looks like differs from one couple to the next—or from one throuple to the next, for that matter. There's a wealth of incredibly sexy things that

---

57   Orenstein.

can happen without a penis penetrating a vagina or anus, and pretending otherwise might net some guys a meagre short-term benefit here and there, but it won't do you or your partners any favours in the grand scheme of things.

Not only is a laser-like focus on penetrative sex narrow-minded and exclusionary, it's also likely to lead to bad sex if and when you actually do get to penetration. For one, penetration isn't feasible for all people—for instance, people affected by vaginismus, people dealing with erectile dysfunction, people with micropenises. Second, people who need more warm-up time to be in the right mood, as well as those who struggle to orgasm from penetrative sex, benefit greatly when things don't focus on penetration to the exclusion of all else.

Lots of people like to think of foreplay—kissing, fingering, oral sex—as an appetizer to be engaged in before the main course. Part of that is that porn typically follows that same narrative arc, if the foreplay stuff shows up at all, but part of it is that penetration is *never* left out. It's not hard to figure out what the star of the show is. Some of it is just that the primacy of penetration is a culturally entrenched narrative, perhaps stemming from the mentality that sex is first and foremost about reproduction, and the fact that we rarely see queer sex depicted in mainstream movies or TV.

If the only sex you hear, see or read about prior to your own first sexual experiences focuses primarily on P-in-V penetration to the exclusion of everything else, it's no surprise that that's what you'll try to emulate when you start having sex.

But most of the sex that we have isn't about reproduction, it's about pleasure—and in fact, many people never have sex for reproduction at all. It may feel counterintuitive, but being able to shift your perception of sex—to make penetrative sex just a part of your sexual buffet—will make you a much, much better sexual partner for a number of reasons.

And I get it, penetration feels awesome, and for many straight guys, it reinforces the dynamic they crave, the one where they're "in control" during sex. And if your mentality is "sex is about having an orgasm, penetration is what makes me orgasm, therefore I will focus on penetration," you are, in a way, thinking logically. It's a very "if A, then B" mentality.

Unfortunately, it's also a very short-sighted way to approach sex. For starters, it completely elides your partner's body, as well as your partner's pleasure. A better formulation might be "sex is about pleasure, both parties enjoying themselves is likely to give me the most amount of pleasure, therefore I will focus on making sure my partner enjoys sex as well."

That's not just a mental thing, either. Sure, some people might not necessarily care, notice or enjoy themselves more if their partner is having a better time, but giving your partner time to get properly lubricated before P-in-V penetration is vital. The difference between sex with someone who's into it and sex with someone who isn't is enormous—and getting to that point of mutual excitement means being sexual without penetration.

It's fair to say that if focusing on penetration can worsen sex, stepping back from that focus and exploring non-penetrative sex can make it better . . . a lot better. That doesn't just mean "more foreplay," though, since it subtly implies that it's less important than what comes after.

Sex that's less focused on penetration is also less likely to be over in a hurry. It's also great news for guys who struggle with erectile dysfunction as the specific hardness of your penis is significantly less important (or possibly not important at all).

The most important thing to realize is that it's incredibly broad, and whatever works for you and/or your partner is worth trying.

You gain nothing by being a selfish sexual partner, but you lose an opportunity to have a more enjoyable experience. Your likelihood of a follow-up encounter drops. And you make the other person less likely to want to engage in fun, casual sex again. Hookups don't happen in a vacuum; every time some other guy treats a woman badly, it impacts the likelihood that she'll say yes when you come knocking.

6

~~a real man doesn't need to~~
wear a bandaid

"Don't go to the hospital. Die. Be a man."

—@bostonbeaman

We learn so many lessons in school that have nothing to do with the curriculum. Schools are also a place where we learn about social dynamics: hierarchy, taboo, in-group vs. out-group.

The phrase "peer pressure" doesn't go nearly far enough: by virtue of representing the majority of most kids' social interactions with others their age, school is a place that teaches you how to be human, the strange math of magnetic pulls exerting themselves, the self forming in fits and starts from lessons learned: don't act like this, don't look like that, don't speak to her, don't laugh at him. Peer pressure isn't a distinct occurrence, a unique phenomenon that acts on you in a visible way—it's the very water you're swimming in.

Because of the way gender functions, it's no surprise, of course, that school is an incredible force in teaching us about how to behave according to our assigned genders.

By the time you show up for your first day of school, you probably have a decent idea of some aspects of gender, but any kid who doesn't hew to the rules will be taught eventually, whether by teachers, or, more often, by the other kids.

I remember clearly a moment in my second or third year of high school when I learned that taking care of your body wasn't considered masculine. I don't mean taking care of your body like pampering yourself—facial creams, moisturizers, massages and oils. I mean taking care of your body like basic first aid.

A boy on the periphery of the popular kids taught me. Let's call him Casey. He was good looking and athletic, but shorter than the other boys, and with a penchant for acting up in class. He'd doctor up a bottle of Liquid Paper to say "squid raper" and look at me expectantly, hoping for a laugh.

We were in gym class, outdoors, having just run around the block, and Casey asked me why I was wearing a bandaid.

"Because I cut myself," I replied. He might as well have asked me why I was wearing shorts and a T-shirt, for all the logic the question seemed to possess.

I don't remember how Casey phrased his response, but I could read between the lines. He was calling me a pussy. He bragged about how he'd walked off a foot injury not long ago that had turned out to be a break. He was so proud of pushing through pain, like he'd been taught to, that he had to pull me down. Wearing a bandaid? Showing the world that I'd been hurt but had remedied the situation? Embarrassing.

It's hard to think of a smaller moment that more perfectly captures the relationship between masculinity and healthcare. A bandaid might be the single most basic unit of medical equipment, something every child is familiar with from before they start school. Stigmatizing the use of one is about as pointless as it gets, particularly when juxtaposed against Casey's very ill-advised approach.

Inherent in his bragging was the contradiction at the heart of so much of contemporary masculinity: the desire to dominate and the desire not to be caught trying. Casey was an athlete, in shape and no stranger to competitive fire. But what approach to sports could you possibly embrace that's more self-sabotaging than intentionally trying to play through pain, minimizing or ignoring serious injuries?

Anyone who knows anything about athletics knows that mishandling an injury in the short-term is far too often a recipe for re-injury in the long-term, whether it be an accumulation of ailments that means your knees are never free from pain or a small but manageable problem becoming much, much worse in an instant due to a single fall or misplaced step.

Pain is the body trying to tell you something. And most people are capable of listening. But like so many other ideologies and religions, masculinity is a belief system that tells you to ignore the body, to impose your sheer force of will upon your physical being, to pretend that the body is just another thing that can be controlled if you're strong enough.

Casey had been brought up within a culture that valorized and propagated the ideals of masculinity, and he understood its teachings well enough to correctly recognize that the bandaid was an emblem of weakness. It was a sissy symbol, denoting too small an injury to be proud of, the kind of thing a real man would walk off.

After Casey's comment, I don't remember if I ripped the bandaid off—surely, by then, the bleeding had stopped; it hadn't been a big cut—but the moment stayed with me, and I remembered it for years afterward when dealing with cuts. This is the way an ideology spreads, like a red stain.

~

Of course, the smallness of that moment between me and Casey makes it a bit laughable, and barely worth dwelling on. But I described it here in detail because it's a very early step on a path that men are encouraged to walk down their whole lives, practically from birth. It's a path of prioritizing a fictional narrative of strength over the simple reality that the human body is a porous, fragile and imperfect organism, and the consequences of that mentality can be far more severe than the mismanagement of small cuts and scrapes, or trying to walk off a bruise that's actually a break: it's a path that ends, far too often, in men dying young. Years if not decades before their time.

The gap between male and female life expectancy—last discussed in Chapter 4—may be stark and easy to see, but it's a complex issue with no clear cure-all. Every person is unique, and each death is too; to attempt to boil each and every death down to one or two things would be reductive and counterproductive.

When a man dies from heart failure in his late 60s, is it a case of random bad luck? Perhaps it was genetic factors—predictable but not controllable. Maybe undue strain from a lifetime of poor stress management or diet or lifestyle choices. Maybe it's a societal or governmental failing: the things that could have saved this man weren't made freely available or promoted to people like him.

Still, it's hard for me to argue that the socialization of young boys to appear strong even when they don't feel strong isn't a significant factor in adult men's resistance to seek medical help when they're ailing, or their reluctance to engage in safer forms of the activities they love. Whether it's skipping the helmet when cycling[58] and the seat belt when driving[59] or, during the pandemic, the reluctance—much more prevalent among men than among women—to wear masks[60] or get vaccinated,[61] in general men seem much

---

58   Taylor & Francis Group, "Many injured US adult cyclists not wearing a helmet: And men are the worst offenders, says new study," *ScienceDaily*, September 13, 2019, https://www.sciencedaily.com /releases/2019/09/190913080738.htm.
59   News staff, "Men less likely to wear seatbelts, more likely to die in crashes: OPP," CityNews, March 22, 2016, https://toronto. citynews.ca/2016/03/22/men-less-likely-to-wear-seatbelts-more -likely-to-die-in-crashes-opp/.
60   Laken Brooks, "Studies Indicate That Men Are Less Likely To Wear Face Masks Than Women. Why?" *Forbes*, August 31, 2021, https://www.forbes.com/sites/lakenbrooks/2021/08/31/macho-men -refused-to-wear-face-masks-but-masculinity-didnt-save-them-from -covid-19/.
61   Angelica Puzio, "Why Is There Such A Gender Gap In COVID-19 Vaccination Rates?" *FiveThirtyEight*, June 22, 2021, https://fivethirtyeight.com/features/why-is-there-such-a-gender-gap -in-covid-19-vaccination-rates/.

less interested in their own safety, and the consequences of that are predictably and horrifyingly deadly.

The guys who die young in one of these situations most likely used to think they were just doing the normal thing—they didn't see the fragility of their bodies, the speed with which death can come crashing into our lives. And when it comes to this mentality, the call is often coming from inside the house. As Andrew Reiner details in a heartbreaking scene in *Better Boys, Better Men*:

> The video was shot on someone's smartphone. The frame is vertical and tight, focusing the entire time on an African American toddler. His shirt is off, and he is sitting on an examination table. A health-care professional is readying a series of vaccinations.
>
> As the boy waits, unsure about what is happening, his father tries to get him ready. "You're looking scared," he says. "You're a big boy, right?"
>
> After the boy receives the first shot, pain registers on his face. The father urges, "Big boy. Big boy." Then his attempt to fortify his son takes on a more serious tone.
>
> "Be a man," the father says.
>
> Over the next few seconds, as the boy's tears increase, something happens.
>
> "The father makes an "Arrgh" noise, which sounds less like a pirate's call and more like a linebacker charging a quarterback. "Big boy," the father says, this time with more urgency.

"You got it. Don't cry. Be a ma—big boy." As the son gets his next vaccination, the father's hand enters the frame. "High five!" No response. The son lapses deeper into tears, and the father bellows, "Say, 'You a man. I'm a man.'"

And then the tension ratchets even higher. The camera zooms in on the toddler's face. Tears are literally streaming off his cheeks. "Say, 'I'm a man,'" the father demands. Off camera, the health-care worker adds, "Say it loud. Say it loud!" The father continues: "Say, 'I'm a man!'"

Through streaming tears, the boy looks back and forth between the two adults. He slaps his right arm against his side, and, then, amid whimpering and a furrowed brow, from somewhere deep within he conjures a gruff, embattled voice. "Ima man!" he yells, his hand pounding his chest.[62]

Scenes like this might not be captured in such detail often, but they are incredibly common. Far too many parents pass this message on to their young boys in some form or other, and even if the parents don't, the rest of the world seems ready to step in and do it for them. This is

---

62   One aspect that Reiner doesn't explore further is, I think, worth addressing. The parent and child in this video are Black. In a racist society, people of colour often feel pressure to push their sons to exhibit traditional masculinity more so than white people. That's not to say that this scene would play out any differently in many white households, just that race is a compounding factor when it comes to gender ideology and norms.

the brainwashing at work: teaching boys to push through pain and fear in the name of "being a man" rather than acknowledging the validity, the reality that being a man doesn't mean pretending there's nothing wrong, but rather being able to deal with the things that are wrong.

~

When I was a kid, my parents got an orange tabby cat I called Cattie. When she died—around when I was six or seven—the asthma that I'd struggled with for years seemed to clear up. My parents got me tested for allergies, which led to the discovery that I'd been allergic to her the whole time. From around that age, I was mostly out of contact with the medical establishment as a whole.

I was proud, for much of my teens and 20s, of how little I went to the doctor. It felt like something impressive about me. When I was 13 or so, I went to the hospital to deal with what seemed like it might be a broken thumb but turned out to be only a sprain, but from then until a trip to get my finger stitched up at 27—following a mishap with a new knife while slicing bread for a post-party grilled cheese on New Year's—excepting regular dentist visits, I hadn't sought out medical care of any kind. No doctor visits, no clinic visits, no hospital visits, no annual checkups. At the time, that was half of my life.

Let me say that again: it was half of my life.

I felt like some sort of medical marvel. When I revealed this fact to the nurse taking care of my sliced-up finger, she chided me, a tired frustration in her voice. But I grinned. I didn't feel naughty, I felt special. I didn't need help, and that made me better than other people.

But it's not like nothing was ever wrong, and it's not like, in being casual about my health, I wasn't being dumb. Living in Quebec, I had access to free healthcare, but during my 20s, I allowed my Medicare card to lapse, going over a year without a valid health card, putting off the relatively simple errand of travelling to a specific government building a half-hour walk at most from my apartment for months on end. Had anything serious happened to me during that period, my life would have been immeasurably more complicated. But I didn't want to think about that kind of thing, and so I shuffled it to the back of my mind.

Part of that was my outsized anxiety around navigating bureaucracy, which I'll delve into a bit more in Chapter 7. But part of it was that, since birth, I'd been told—implicitly and explicitly—like everyone else raised within the narrow strictures of masculinity, that seeking help was bad, that weakness was bad, that taking precautions to protect myself was bad.

~

By this point, there's no shortage of evidence that men have an unhealthy relationship to their physical health. Study after study, actuarial table after actuarial table, country after country, generation after generation. As far back as 2008, people were writing things like this quote by Guy Garcia from his book *The Decline of Men*:

It's been known for a long time that women out-
live men by an average of five years, and until
recently few people wondered why. But medical advocates and scientists are beginning to ask
questions that would have been unthinkable just
a few years ago: Are men getting sicker than they
should? Are men dying younger than they need
to? Are we even looking at the right symptoms?
And what, if anything, can be done about it?[63]

The jury is in—men visit their doctors less often,[64] injure
themselves more frequently and seriously,[65] engage in more
violent and risky behaviour,[66] smoke more,[67] drink more,[68]

63   Guy Garcia, *The Decline of Men: How the American Male Is
Tuning Out, Giving Up, and Flipping Off His Future* (New York:
Harper, 2008).
64   Batya Swift Yasgur, "Why Are Men Less Likely to See a
Doctor?" WebMD, July 6, 2021, https://www.webmd.com/men/news
/20210706/men-less-likely-to-see-doctor-study.
65   J.R. Udry, "Why Are Males Injured More Than Females?"
Injury Prevention 4 (1998): 94–95.
66   Rache l A. Knoblach. "Men Riskier, More Aggressive,"
Encyclopedia of Evolutionary Psychological Science, https://doi.
org/10.1007/978-3-319-16999-6_1674-1.
67   National Institute on Drug Abuse, *Are There Gender
Differences in Tobacco Smoking?*, April 12, 2021, https://nida.nih.
gov/publications/research-reports/tobacco-nicotine-e-cigarettes/
are-there-gender-differences-in-tobacco-smoking.
68   Aaron M. White, "Gender Differences in the Epidemiology
of Alcohol Use and Related Harms in the United States," *Alcohol
Research Current Reviews* 40, no. 2 (October 29, 2020), https://arcr
.niaaa.nih.gov/women-and-alcohol/gender-differences-epidemiology
-alcohol-use-and-related-harms-united-states.

do more drugs,[69] eat less health-conscious diets[70] and die younger.[71]

Yet when it comes to medical science, men are at an advantage. The majority of doctors are men, and though women have cared for the sick in myriad ways throughout history, in much of modernity they were officially barred from practising medicine; it's only in recent decades that women MDs have become common-place.[72] As a result of the male domination and baked-in sexism of the medical field, women are understudied, undertreated, and often totally dismissed. (And care is generally even worse for women who are further away from the white, cishet, thin, able-bodied "norm.") Women, for instance, are at a much greater risk of dying from heart attacks than men are, because they often present different symptoms than men.[73] When women complain of pain, doctors are also much less likely to administer painkillers or otherwise address the problem

69   National Institute on Drug Abuse.

70   Jennifer L. Black and Jean-Michel Billette, "Fast Food in Canada: Who Is Eating the Most?" BC Food Web, February 18, 2020, https://bcfoodweb.ca/briefs/fast-food-canada-who-eating-most.

71   Bridget Murray-Law, "Why Do Men Die Earlier?" *Monitor on Psychology* 42, no. 6 (June 2011), https://www.apa.org/monitor/2011/06/men-die.

72   Farrah Jarral, "No Scrubs: How Women Had to Fight to Become Doctors," *The Guardian*, September 26, 2016, https://www.theguardian.com/lifeandstyle/2016/sep/26/no-scrubs-how-women-had-to-fight-to-become-doctors.

73   Barbara Sadick, "Women Die from Heart Attacks More Often Than Men. Here's Why—and What Doctors Are Doing About It," *Time*, April 1, 2019, https://time.com/5499872/women-heart-disease/.

than when men do.[74] The assumption is that if a man is hurting enough to be moved to complain, it must be really serious—but women are hysterical; they'll complain about anything.

Despite these advantages to women, men are in much worse health, overall, and, again, die younger—much younger. Why? For all of the barriers to their getting proper care, women have one major advantage: they take their own symptoms seriously. Men getting sicker and dying younger is more or less what you'd expect from a cohort of people who are systematically brainwashed as children to believe that admitting something is wrong is the worst thing you can possibly do. Then you get things like these results of a 2019 survey by the Cleveland Clinic that asked men about their relationship to healthcare: "about two-thirds (65%) of men tend to wait as long as possible to see their doctor if they have any health symptoms or an injury," "one-fifth (20%) of men admit they have not been completely honest with their doctor before," and "two-fifths (37%) of men who admit they haven't been completely honest with their doctor withheld information because they knew something was wrong but weren't ready to face the diagnosis and/or would rather not know if they have any health issues."[75]

But when you refuse to acknowledge a problem, it

74   Jennifer Billock, "Pain Bias: The Health Inequality Rarely Discussed," BBC, May 22, 2018, https://www.bbc.com/future/article/20180518-the-inequality-in-how-women-are-treated-for-pain.
75   Cleveland Clinic, "2019 Cleveland Clinic MENtion It® Survey Results Overview," 2019, https://newsroom.clevelandclinic.org/wp-content/uploads/sites/4/2019/09/2019-Cleveland-Clinic-MENtion-It-Survey-Results-Overview.pdf.

doesn't go away—and in terms of health issues, it often metastasizes.

~

These days, when I think about the boys I went to school with, I don't think about Casey. I think about Derek.

In high school terms, Derek had it all—he was tall and muscular, perfectly tanned, an athlete, a popular kid. He had a winning smile, and the gossip in my final year was that one of the new, younger teachers was openly hitting on him in class. Though that last example is more troubling to me now in retrospect, at the time, from my perspective near the bottom of the pecking order, Derek seemed to be living a charmed life.

Then, one night a few years after we graduated, he was killed while hanging out in the countryside with three other high school pals. They'd been drinking, the driver lost control of the van, and Derek was ejected—he hadn't been wearing his seat belt. The van landed on him. His friends weren't able to get it off.

The death haunted me. No one that young should ever die, but he was the first person I knew to die young, and one of the first people I knew who died, period. The incongruity of his sudden and tragic demise was hard to shake. I dealt with it the way immature kids deal with things they can't process—by joking about it with another kid from our year. Just things like "remember derek, lol." A few years later, in college, in creative writing, I submitted an "experimental poem" that was just a series of posts people had made on Derek's Facebook wall after he passed. There was something in the rawness of the mourning I couldn't turn away from, the clichéd phrases alive with the fire of grief. I'd never personally experienced that gut-wrenching sorrow, and honestly, I still haven't. I'm lucky not to.

On some level, I could never understand why Derek hadn't buckled up that night, or why he and his friends had ended up in a moving vehicle driven by someone who'd been drinking. My parents didn't have a car when I was growing up, so going for a drive was a rare occasion—taxi rides to the airport and car rentals for trips out of the city, mostly. I took their warnings to wear my seat belt seriously, like they were a matter of life and death. Because even when they aren't—which is most of the time—when they are, you don't get an extra second to snap the buckle shut.

On another level, though, I understood all too well why Derek hadn't worn his seat belt. He was a young man who'd moved through life in a body that, at least from my vantage point, was perfect. If he'd known pain, he'd known healing. He'd known strength, rather than weakness. He'd known confidence rather than fear. Most likely—like so many boys and men do—he'd thought that going out of his way to be safe would make him look weak. Even if it was a small thing, like putting on a helmet or buckling a seat belt.[76]

Of course, there are no situations in life where a bandaid will save your life. That's why we call them bandaid solutions—they're not for the serious things. But adopting a different approach to little gestures of safety is step one in an overall approach to your physical health that can easily end up saving your life.

So what does wearing a bandaid look like, writ large, in the lives of men? What can you do today to start taking your health seriously? How can you develop a healthier relationship to your body, one based on care and attentiveness rather than trying to push through discomforts small and large to suit a narrative?

The first step, I think, is to disabuse yourself of the notion that strength means ignoring pain, downplaying weakness or pretending nothing's wrong with your body. Let me say that again a little clearer: ignoring pain doesn't mean you're strong. Pain and weakness are not the same thing. This may sound self-evident, but so many boys are reared to believe the opposite, and the results are heartbreaking.

---

76   I want to acknowledge that there's nothing explicitly tying Derek's death to masculine ideology. That's one of the tricky parts about so many young men's untimely deaths — there's no blinking neon sign linking them to unhealthy things they were taught about manhood growing up, implicitly and/or explicitly. In Derek's case, it may well have been unrelated. But when we have a culture where boys are encouraged not to take precautions, and some of them go on to die preventable deaths, I believe that arguing against the connection only does a disservice to the goal of preventing tragedy.

So long as you keep valorizing that kind of mentality, and valorizing people who live it, you're going to wind up reflecting that same mentality back onto yourself and it will colour and infect how you see and treat your own body. So long as you belittle and mock those who fall short of the invented ideal of strength—the pro athletes who struggle with injuries, boxers who lose fights, seniors past their physical primes, young people with disabilities—you'll be doing your best to distance your own body's weakness from theirs.

In time, every body fails. That's what death means—no one is invincible. And you can argue that it's better to die young and in full possession of your faculties than to survive for more than a century while slowly withering away, but that's not the dichotomy that taking care of your health presents: men don't just drop dead suddenly, they also suffer from health conditions that impair and impede their abilities to live the active lives they were used to in their youths. Genuine health isn't a question of quantity, it's a question of quality. That better quality so often begets higher quantity is just a bonus.

When you begin from a starting point that recognizes the body's inherent fallibility, and that doesn't judge someone for a body that's vulnerable, the concept of pretending to be OK when you aren't stops making sense entirely. You're comfortable calling the doctor to schedule a checkup, comfortable researching symptoms when something seems like it's up, comfortable talking to other people about a feeling of discomfort you're experiencing. You're comfortable wearing a bandaid over a little cut. That comfort alone won't save your life, but it allows you to be in a position to catch early warning signs much more easily than if you treat anything wrong with your body as something that needs to be ignored, suppressed or papered over.

7

~~tough men don't need to~~

see a shrink

"Men, after all, hate women so that they don't have
to hate themselves."

—Katherine Angel, *Tomorrow Sex Will Be Good*
Again

A boy is molested in Arkansas. A trans woman is
murdered in New Orleans. A father is stabbed to
death in Toronto. A workplace is shot up in New Jersey.
A string of rapes goes unsolved in British Columbia. A
baby is kidnapped in Los Angeles. Welcome to the headlines—ground zero for male mental health.

Have you ever come across the phrase "male mental
health" before? Maybe in an article in an online magazine
or in a segment on the radio? It's a fun little three-word
number that encapsulates an astonishing amount of information about the society we live in. It's wild, because every
gruesome story you've ever heard, almost without fail, can
be chalked up to male mental health in some form or other:
men enraged about a recent firing, men despondent over

a breakup, men apoplectic with anger about a childhood wound that never truly healed. A drumbeat of lost men losing it all over again.

While it's a societal crisis we can't afford to ignore one second longer, male mental health is also an incredibly vague concept. How does one conceive of the relative soundness of mind of roughly half the population, exactly? If half the population is doing something or feeling something, isn't the other half just as weird for not doing or feeling that thing?

And yet some things feel concretely like poor male mental health, and outbursts of violence like those I've just mentioned are chief among them. As I'll explore more in Chapter 8, male violence isn't a mental health issue— at least, not first and foremost. Whether it's punching someone in a bar, robbing a convenience store at gunpoint or raping their spouse, most men who commit violent acts, as you may well know, are simply acting out pre-existing scripts for men and have nothing exceptionally strange or off about them. From a mental health perspective, they are probably not much different than you or the men you know—rather, they are men who believe that violence is an appropriate solution to a problem they're facing. In this, they may be wrong, but they're not the only ones. Violence is one of the primary languages of masculinity, if not *the* primary one, and there's no reason to believe the majority of the men who engage with it have a diagnosable condition of any kind.

When you have a culture where some people are more likely to be violent, and are less likely to be in therapy, taking mood medication or otherwise being in touch with their emotions in a grounded way, well, you've set the scene for a culture where acts of violence by those same people are so common they almost fade into the background, are so common they almost become the background itself.

Of course, mental health issues can strike people all over the world—young and old, rich and poor, healthy and not. They impact people regardless of their political leanings and religious beliefs, and are essentially agnostic when it comes to ethnicity or gender. And yet, it's hard to ignore the fact that mental health struggles impact cis men much differently than they do women and trans people. That's why we have the phrase "male mental health" to begin with.

Let's review the facts. Men are less likely to seek out help,[77] which means they're less likely to end up in therapy and less likely to be on medication. The fact that they're more violent—and more likely to be perceived as violent—means that they're more likely to be perceived as needing police intervention when going through mental health episodes, which means they're more likely to be killed or incarcerated. Then there's suicide, which men die from at much, much higher rates than women;[78] in the U.S., men's suicide rate is three-and-a-half times that of women. Or murder, which is even more gender-slanted—nearly 90%

77   Lea Winerman, "Helping Men to Help Themselves," *Monitor on Psychology* 36, no. 7 (June 2005), https://www.apa.org/monitor/jun05/helping.
78   Ann Matturro Gault, "My Dad Died from Depression: Paul McGregor on Rising Male Suicide Rates," Psycom, May 14, 2019, https://www.psycom.net/depression-in-men-male-suicide-rates.

of homicide offenders are male.[79] Or even houselessness, long tied to mental health concerns, which is overwhelmingly a male issue, with a recent U.S. Department of Housing and Urban Development report suggesting over three-fifths of unhoused people in the United States are men.[80]

These aren't random statistics—they're logical outcomes of an incredible disparity in how we socialize children in vastly different ways depending on which genitals they have, which includes how to handle negative emotions that occur naturally, to some degree or other, in every human being's life: fear, anger, jealousy, worry, anxiety, sadness, regret. Far too many boys are, essentially, emotionally illiterate, as psychologists Dan Kindlon and Michael Thompson write in their 1999 book, *Raising Cain: Protecting the Emotional Life of Boys*. This isn't a fact of nature; it's something that can be taught, if you're willing to learn:

> A large part of our work with boys and men is to help them understand their emotional life and develop an emotional vocabulary. We begin by helping them increase their clarity about their feelings and those of others—recognizing them, naming them, and learning where they come from. . . .

79   Alexia Cooper and Erica L. Smith, *Homicide Trends in the United States, 1980–2008* U.S. Department of Justice, November 2011, https://bjs.ojp.gov/content/pub/pdf/htus8008.pdf.
80   National Alliance to End Homelessness, *Demographic Data Project*, 2018, https://endhomelessness.org/demographic-data-project-gender-and-individual-homelessness/.

This process is much like learning to read. First we must master the letters and sounds of the alphabet, then use that knowledge to decode words and sentences. As we begin to comprehend and appreciate increasingly complex thoughts, we are able to communicate more effectively with others. Eventually, reading connects us to a larger world, beyond our own, of experiences and ideas.

Similarly, learning emotional literacy involves recognizing the look and feel of our emotions, then using this skill to better understand ourselves and others. We learn to appreciate life's emotional complexity, and this enhances all our professional and personal relationships, helping us to strengthen the connections that enrich our lives.

We build emotional literacy, first, by being able to identify and name our emotions; second, by recognizing the emotional content of voice and facial expression, or body language; and third, by understanding the situations or reactions that produce emotional states. By this we mean becoming aware of the link between loss and sadness, between frustration and anger, or threats to pride or self-esteem and fear.[81]

~

---

81   Dan Kindlon and Michael Thompson, *Raising Cain: Protecting the Emotional Life of Boys* (New York: Ballantine Books, 1999).

It's too expensive. I'm fine, I don't need it. It's for weirdos,
for psychos. I tried it once and it didn't do anything for
me. Waste of time. There's no therapists in my area. That's
for people with real problems. Talking on a couch to some
old guy about your feelings? Sissy shit. No room in my
schedule. The gym is my therapy.

Guys have lots of arguments as to why they're not seeing
a therapist. Press an average guy who's not in therapy for
a little bit about why, and one of those responses is bound
to pop up, if not multiple. Hell, for some guys, maybe all
of them do. But in these replies, it's hard not to hear a little
kid getting defensive when confronted about something in
the schoolyard, or maybe being asked about his homework
by an adult. Replies like those feel thin, and smokescreeny.
They feel like what they are—excuses, not reasons.

The real reason most guys aren't seeing a therapist isn't
complicated. It's because they're scared.

That's not to say that some of the more bread-and-butter
reasons aren't valid concerns. Some guys legitimately
don't have room in their budget for therapy. Some guys
live places where there aren't any therapists nearby, or the
closest ones aren't accepting new clients. Some guys—
particularly boys and men of colour—might struggle to
find a therapist who can speak to the particular issues they
face. But it's also true that men who are scared to genuinely
confront their mental health issues use these reasons to
get out of doing the psychological and emotional heavy
lifting that therapy entails. There's a reason people use
the phrase "confronting your demons" when talking about
therapy. It's not easy. If you're doing it right, you often

come out of sessions feeling like you've been through the wringer. You might need to take a walk, or a nap, or eat some comfort food afterward. You might feel drained. You might even cry.

But guess what? The things worth doing in life are never especially easy, and long-term growth always comes with a short-term cost. You don't get your dream body by hitting up the gym every two weeks and lifting ten-pound weights for half an hour, or going for a brief jog once a month, and you don't get your dream psyche by coasting through life, burying your feelings and only opening up when you're drunk or at your wits' end. Whether one-on-one or in a group setting, therapy— talking about your feelings, your problems, your goals and your wounds—is the psychological version of a workout routine. Some therapy is better than no therapy, and not all therapy needs to be expensive.

And if it is costly in a literal, immediate sense, at least it's something that benefits you for decades afterward. Not going to therapy, on the other hand, saves you money—but for millions and millions of men, it comes with costs of its own, and those costs are sometimes financial ones. If you blow up a relationship with the person of your dreams because you're not emotionally mature enough, there's no dollar amount to quantify what you've lost. But if you break your laptop in a fit of rage because you never learned how to process your anger, well, there's a literal price tag on that, and it's more expensive than a few therapy sessions.

~

Mental health issues strike at the rich and poor alike, although they are no more a great leveller than anything else—in a capitalist world, if you have more money, you can deal with problems more easily. But it is fascinating to read things like author and graphic novelist Neil Gaiman's account of meeting another famous Neil—which he posted on his Tumblr—to see that success is no guarantee of self-confidence, fame no guarantee of self-esteem.

> Some years ago, I was lucky enough [to be] invited to a gathering of great and good people: artists and scientists, writers and discoverers of things. And I felt that at any moment they would realise that I didn't qualify to be there, among these people who had really done things.
>
> On my second or third night there, I was standing at the back of the hall, while a musical entertainment happened, and I started talking to a very nice, polite, elderly gentleman about several things, including our shared first name. And then he pointed to the hall of people, and said words to the effect of, "I just look at all these people, and I think, what the heck am I doing here? They've made amazing things. I just went where I was sent."
>
> And I said, "Yes. But you were the first man on the moon. I think that counts for something."
>
> And I felt a bit better. Because if Neil Armstrong felt like an imposter, maybe *everyone* did. Maybe there weren't any grown-ups, only people who had worked hard and also got lucky and were slightly

out of their depth, all of us doing the best job we could, which is all we can really hope for.[82]

Of course, it's easy to imagine the inverse of this scenario, as well—two white men at a conference full of successful people trying to outdo each other with their boasts and their wit. To some degree, self-deprecation can also be more male posturing, substituting an extreme narrative rather than having the confidence to get into the weeds of the self and try to see things as they really are—complex, both good and bad, but rarely, if ever, utterly perfect or purely horrific.

From that perspective, both overconfidence and its complete absence constitute what bell hooks would call a mask: "Learning to wear a mask ... is the first lesson in patriarchal masculinity that a boy learns," she writes in her 2004 book, *The Will to Change: Men, Masculinity, and Love.* "He learns that his core feelings cannot be expressed if they do not conform to the acceptable behaviors sexism defines as male."

In the next sentence, hooks explores the stakes of this learning with a clarity that many so-called gender experts shy away from: "Asked to give up the true self in order to realize the patriarchal ideal, boys learn self-betrayal early and are rewarded for these acts of soul murder."[83]

---

82   Neil Gaiman, "The Neil Story (with Additional Footnote),"
May 17, 2017, https://journal.neilgaiman.com/2017/05/the-neil-story-with-additional-footnote.html.
83   bell hooks, *The Will to Change: Men, Masculinity, and Love* (New York: Washington Square Press, 2004).

Read that again. When you substitute part of your true self, part of your genuine personality, she's saying, with chunks of a false ideal, an imagined picture of who society thinks you're supposed to be, you're killing a part of your soul.

~

Once you've seen a therapist more than a dozen or so times, or been on mood medication for a few months or more, it can be easy to sound like you've had your shit together since Day 1—you simply knew you needed help and you got it and it fixed your life. It's easy, at a certain step of the process of figuring out how to deal with your own mental health, to act very blasé and even a bit cocky about it. I don't want that to be what you take away from this chapter, though.

The truth is, despite some on-again, off-again stints in therapy in my early 20s, I didn't genuinely start taking my mental health seriously until six months or so before my 30th birthday. That's when, at the urging of my then-girlfriend, I called my doctor and asked if he would write me a prescription for anti-anxiety medication. He did, and I started taking it, and that changed a lot of things in a big way in a relatively short period of time.

But even framing it like that is a bit dishonest. It makes it look like the whole thing was fated to work out. The truth is, at the time, I had no real idea how things would go, and even if I felt a certain clarity regarding wanting to try medication, the simple process of making that call, getting the prescription, filling it and beginning to take the meds felt arduous, daunting and overlong—to say nothing of the first few weeks on the drug, which, as its impact on my brain began to be felt, were a grey blur of much worse depression than I was used to, before ultimately stabilizing into something workable, something much like it had been before, only better.

The truth is, I'd been struggling with anxiety issues for my whole life, but in the few years prior to that phone call, it had started to become increasingly obvious that it wasn't just a quirk of personality or a fact of nature, but something that was holding me back from living the life I wanted to live— a set of symptoms that could be alleviated, if not erased, with medical help.

No longer was I willing to just accept that socializing was a nerve-wracking experience that everyone else seemed to enjoy but that terrified me. No longer was I happy to sit idly by while less-senior coworkers got promoted above me thanks to their ability to show up on time every day, complete their assignments by the stated due dates and respond to pressing emails in minutes instead of hours or days. No longer was I content to live a life that just felt hamstrung at almost every turn by the presence of an invisible barrier that other people didn't seem to face.

The eureka moment for me came one night around March 2018, as I cast my thoughts back to a Friday afternoon at work a few months prior. Working at a men's website meant that there was always a fair amount of alcohol in the office, between the beer fridge we had installed and the bottles of hard liquor almost every senior employee seemed to have at their desks. As a confirmed lightweight, though, I'd discovered a long time ago that even drinking a small amount at work made it near-impossible for me to get any writing or editing done, and so I typically abstained from any proffered bottles until I was sure my work was finished. For whatever reason, this particular Friday, I had cracked open a cold one and let the buzz settle in. And it was to my surprise, an hour and a half later or so, that I found I'd just rattled off replies to five or six unread emails I'd been avoiding, clustered at the top of my inbox, taunting me, some for as many as a week or more, probably.

That March night, walking through a park with my then-girlfriend, talking about feeling blocked and stuck at work, I remembered the fateful winter Friday where I'd responded to all those scary emails in one go. How easy it had felt. And of course, I realized, it was the beer buzz that helped me do it—it got me to a place where my inhibitions were lowered. I realized, in that moment, with crystal clarity, that the problem wasn't insurmountable, wasn't an immutable, innate part of me—it was something that could be altered with chemicals. In decades past, different versions of me might have simply become alcoholics in order to function. I'm glad, in that moment, that what I did was shed my reluctance around pharmaceuticals and set out to get a prescription from my doctor. This book would probably not exist otherwise.

A few months after getting on anti-anxiety meds, I started seeing a therapist on a weekly basis. About a year later, I finally talked to my doctor about my lifelong issues with distraction and procrastination and got a prescription for ADHD medication. The years since I started anti-anxiety meds have been the most emotionally stable and productive of my life. That first decision made the ones after it that much easier. Of course, I know not everyone's story works like this—not everyone has a family doctor they can call, not everyone can afford therapy or medication and, if you live in the United States, not everyone has medical insurance. But there's a difference between not seeking out medical care because there are concrete barriers to accessing it and not seeking out medical care because of barriers in your self-perception.

~

It's tempting, at times, to conceive of human history as a march forward, a linear progression, a long, slow process of improvement. We live longer now, don't we? We have the internet, and microwaves, and airplanes. But of course, there's a big difference between technological progress and overall quality of life, and the passage of time has a funny way of worsening things in some ways while improving them in others. Would a simple goat-herd somewhere in eighth-century Europe really want to jump forward to the early 20th century, just in time to be conscripted into World War I, with its technological marvels like mustard gas and machine guns? It's not hard to find viral tweets these days begging for a return to a simpler life, before things like credit scores and the gig economy existed, and perhaps even before the invention of agriculture, period.

So it is with certain conceptions of masculinity. Whether you imagine that the contemporary way of being a man is the best way or the only way, rarely does anyone posit that there used to be better ways of being a man—and if they do, it's usually simply to exclaim that today's men are barely men at all, considering how soft they are. And yet, as Steve Biddulph explores in *The New Manhood*, the 2010 reissue of his 1994 book *Manhood*, contemporary masculinity does lack certain more nuanced understandings that have existed in the past. Consider this passage, where he talks about the importance of accepting your emotions:

> Denying your feelings is not always a bad thing: it serves an important evolutionary purpose. If you are a soldier pinned down by machine-gun fire on D-Day, with comrades dying all around you, then getting in touch with your feelings might not be a good idea. Likewise if you are unemployed in the Great Depression, with children hungry and depending on you. But denial is meant to be a short-term strategy, not a way of life. Older and wiser cultures knew this, and deliberately built in ways to help men let go of pain and move on.
>
> Near Taupo in New Zealand, hidden away from the tourist traps and fancy hotels, a small Maori-owned hot spring lies at the head of a small valley. A creek runs over a scalding, bubbling

area of volcanic mud and rocks, then re-enters the forest. There, in a leafy glade, a hot, steaming waterfall dives over a small cliff. This was a sacred place, where warriors, returning from battle, washed away the hate, fear, and bloodiness of war, and became human again. As they did so, they grieved for dead comrades, for the pain and awfulness of killing. They wept and cried out under the torrent of heated water. The women sang to them, and welcomed them back into the peaceful world of the community and the family. The gods had taken away their pain, rage, and grief.[84]

Does that sound like anything you hear about today? Group cry-ins after exhausting, tortuous experiences? A sacred, special place for releasing your hurt and your trauma? The closest contemporary equivalent might be a rage room. To whatever extent past humans understood that letting your feelings out is important regardless of your gender or your genitalia, we've largely lost that in contemporary Western culture. It's time to start getting it back. And while we do need cultural-level systemic change, for now, getting it back starts with individual choices. Hence the title of this chapter.

So when I say see a shrink, I don't mean there's only one way to do that. I don't mean Freudian analysis,

84 Steve Biddulph, *The New Manhood: The Handbook for a New Kind of Man* (Warriewood, New South Wales: Finch Publishing, 2010).

psychotherapy, cognitive behavioural therapy or couples therapy only.

In a 2021 *MEL* magazine article about the infamous "men will literally [do anything] instead of going to therapy" meme, writer Miles Klee notes that therapy is "not a magic solution for every bad man."[85] It's not a magic solution for every man, either, but he's right, of course—for a complex problem like toxic masculinity, there's no such thing as a one-size-fits-all solution, and anyone claiming otherwise is either not thinking about the issue very much or actively lying to you.

But that also doesn't mean that the world wouldn't be a better place if men started taking their emotional and psychological selves much more seriously, such as by seeing licensed mental health professionals, in some capacity, on at least a semi-regular basis, at least for a little while.

So when I say see a shrink, what I mean is take concrete, intentional, serious steps to address your own mental health, within your budget and your abilities, no matter how difficult it might feel to you in the moment. Because your baseline, as a man, may be normal, but it's not healthy. As hooks said, if you've been socialized as a man in contemporary society, you're almost certainly a victim of some degree of soul murder. Things might *feel* fine, but if you're emotionally illiterate, then at least one thing *is* wrong. And because they're scared to seem weak, far

---

85   Miles Klee, "This Meme Literally Won't Get Men into Therapy," *MEL*, https://melmagazine.com/en-us/story/men-will-literally-therapy-meme.

too many men minimize or ignore when things actually *do* seem wrong, as I explored at length in Chapter 6. The consequences of doing that with your physical health can be deadly, but they can be just as devastating if you do it with your mental health. You don't need to exhibit the stereotypical signs that some people associate with mental health issues—things like hearing voices, seeing things or having multiple personalities—to qualify as someone who struggles with them.

So: see someone. Do something about it. That could be group therapy, which a 2017 study suggests men may prefer to psychotherapy.[86] That could be traditional talk therapy, whether in person or digital, as telehealth alternatives have become increasingly popular in recent years. That could be seeking out a diagnosis or prescription from a doctor or psychiatrist if you think you may have a diagnosable mental health issue. It could just be talking to people you're close to about how you're doing, how you're really feeling, rather than staying at the surface and pretending everything's fine, like you learned to as a boy. Because whether or not things get bad enough to land you in a headline like one of those at the beginning of the chapter, male mental health is worth taking seriously.

86   Louise Liddon, Roger Kingerlee and John A. Barry, "Gender differences in preferences for psychological treatment, coping strategies, and triggers to help-seeking," *British Journal of Clinical Psychology*, July 9, 2017, https://bpspsychub.onlinelibrary.wiley.com/doi/abs/10.1111/bjc.12147.

8

~~a real man should never~~
walk away from a fight

"As endless epics, sagas, and eddas attest, heroes become heroes by making others small."

—David Graeber, *Debt*

One of the saddest cultural shifts the United States has seen in the 21st century is the absolute explosion of mass shootings. In 1999, when two students shot and killed 13 people at Columbine High School in Littleton, Colorado, the very concept of the school shooting was enough to sustain the nation's attention for months on end, prompting changes and debates and discussions that reverberated for years.

These days, a school shooting that left over a dozen dead would barely be in the news cycle for a week. In the United States, there's a mass shooting, on average, every single day.[87]

---

87 Júlia Ledur, Kate Rabinowitz and Artur Galocha, "There have been over 300 mass shootings so far in 2022," *Washington Post*, June 2, 2022, https://www.washingtonpost.com/nation/2022/06/02/mass-shootings-in-2022/.

144

Of course, the discussions around these horrific events are tragic in their own way, each one growing and fading and dying just like the last: with calls for gun control, with discussions of male mental health, with insisting we don't name or publicize the killer so as not to inspire copycats, so as to keep the focus on the victims. Though you may hear it less often lately, in the midst of these carbon-copy conversations, for a long time the National Rifle Association and its advocates were fond of saying, "Guns don't kill people—people do."

They're wrong.

People don't kill people, stories do. Think of all the people in the world—with guns or without—who never kill another person. It's a lot of people. Think of all the women who never kill another person. It's almost all of them. Think of all the men who never kill another person—it's still the majority of them; though murderers, soldiers and people who commit manslaughter are all much more likely to be men, they're still in the minority. Think of all the mentally ill people who never kill or harm another person.

That's where stories come in. Stories that say: the other person deserves it. Stories that say: she can't get away with this. Stories that say: he insulted your honour. Or moments where there's a gap between the story and the lived reality. If the story you grew up believing is that you should be the most important person in every room you're in, and the lived reality you're experiencing is that you're never that, grabbing a gun and walking into a room full of unarmed people is a pretty effective way to instantly become the most important person in the room.

Stories are powerful.

That's something storytellers' lives and livelihoods depend on. If stories *didn't* have the potential to change the world—or to at least make or break the few hours you spend in a movie theatre, the summer weekend you spend wrapped up in a pulpy novel, the three months you spend working on a production of a Shakespeare play in high school—we would have stopped telling them long ago.

But we didn't; if anything, stories have proliferated, evolved and intensified. Porn has plots to make it hotter, video games have cut scenes to make them meaningful, albums have skits between the songs, film franchises have novel adaptations to flesh out their cinematic universes. Everywhere you turn, executives are trying to adapt board games into movies, nerds are writing fanfiction about their favourite TV shows, music videos are as densely plotted as a Broadway show. We are addicted to stories.

And look—it makes sense. Humans are social animals, whose oldest traditions, as far as we can tell, involve telling each other tales. Narrative is how we understand the world we inhabit. As the late essayist Joan Didion famously put it, "we tell ourselves stories in order to live."[88] That sounds nice on the surface, but it also carries a lurking menace. Didion understood that that's not always a healthy relationship, that it often means we tell ourselves *lies* in order to live. When your foundational story starts feeling

---

88   Joan Didion, "The White Album," *The White Album* (New York: Simon & Schuster, 1979).

less and less true, when the fabric of your reality starts to grow thin and tear, where do you turn?

Over the past few decades, jobs, money, privilege and power have ceased to be a reliable source of self-esteem for men, particularly white men. But today's crop was raised on the same stories: told that they were the heroes, told that they were better, bottle-fed that lie from birth onwards. They've seen themselves saving the world so many times they couldn't not believe it.

But things changed, at some point. Today's crop is facing a different reality than yesterday's; a reality that's a little bit narrower for them, a little bit thinner. Most of them are still doing fine. But not all of them are managing. Some of them are starting to feel like they've been left behind. They have begun to be told—explicitly at times, implicitly more often—that they can no longer be the hero. In addition to those who haven't been able to get the promotion they wanted, there are those who don't even get the job in the first place. Not necessarily because they're white men; more likely because those jobs just aren't there anymore.

They've been automated out of existence—by software or hardware or both. They've been sent elsewhere. They've been compressed down from something it took 20 people to do to something it takes one person to do. Or else the culture's shifted, taking the public's taste for something with it, so the market's shifted, so the layoffs.

Or worse—the work still needs to be done, same as before, but now you're a tenuously employed contractor scraping together pennies for this week's groceries instead of a unionized, salaried employee putting away money for retirement. And wages aren't keeping pace with inflation, while housing costs skyrocket.

So these men haven't been able to buy a house, maybe won't ever be able to. They haven't been able to lock down a servile, child-bearing wife like their forefathers did, because those women are competing with them in the workforce, or getting post-graduate degrees, or dating women and trans people instead, or just not looking for a man who can't cook or clean or bring flowers home to save his life.

So they never became husbands. They might have a child from some ill-advised hookup, but they never became patriarchs, handing down names and tools and advice and heirlooms.

They never became anything: they were sons then; they're sons now too. That's why we call them failsons—not only have they not improved, they've worsened; fruit gone rotten with age, attracting flies.

These men know they can't be the hero anymore—they come up against the wall of that every day. But they were told they were special, told they meant something, told that to let someone else lead was to admit defeat. So they have made an ugly choice: rather than settle for supporting roles, many of them have chosen to be anti-heroes.

~

If you've spent any time in comment sections, on message boards, or on the cursed app known as Twitter, you may be aware that the modern internet is a wailing chorus of male anger.

There's even an adage about this: "Don't read the comments." It's a sort of generally accepted fact that, where people are allowed to voice their opinions, the opinions will be bad, often horrifically so. And, as the numbers like those in one German study from 2022 show,[89] and as you may have experienced yourself, the majority of these comments are coming from men. Men love to get angry online, to comment, reply and email their anger out in volcanic waves of hatred whenever they perceive someone crossing them—whether that's a direct insult, the statement of an opposing viewpoint or, often, simply someone they dislike choosing to exist at all.

But what gets me is how the men who spend the most time fighting in the muck and mire of the online gender discourse seem to insist on harkening back to an old-world model of masculinity—one that they then eschew in favour of being, well, whiny crybabies. What solemn grandfather would look at the unfolding of Gamergate and proudly nod? What stoic John Wayne figure would spend his nights doxxing feminists? Can you imagine James Bond on 4chan? Getting mad online about women you've never met is possibly the least traditionally manly thing you can do—and yet the men who seem to care most about the

---

89   Constanze Küchler, Anke Stoll, Marc Ziegele and Teresa K. Naab, "Gender-Related Differences in Online Comment Sections: Findings From a Large-Scale Content Analysis of Commenting Behavior," *Social Science Computer Review*, February 2022, https://doi.org/10.1177/08944393211052042.

sanctity of these outdated ideals of masculinity are the ones who crow loudest and shrillest about them, rather than spending their time actually embodying the ideals they claim to value.

It's a byproduct of this training that they received growing up, that all boys do to varying extents, that insists that winning is paramount, losing is anathema and fighting is the way to bridge the difference. The idea that you can walk away from confrontation, or that you can be wrong or outmaneuvered and still hold your head high, seems so rare that when it does pop up people feel the need to make a big deal about it. *Wow, a logical debate among adults handled in a polite manner! Upvotes all 'round.*

But if you can never be vulnerable—if you can never admit you don't know something, can never admit you can't do something, can never admit you were wrong, what kind of person are you? Either you're an omniscient, omnipotent, infallible god who's rationally responding to his perfectness, or you're a crazy person. The late anthropologist David Graeber, who I cited in Chapter 3, writing in his 2011 book, *Debt: The First 5,000 Years*, about past societies who glorified so-called "men of honor," frames it this way: "Men of honor tend to combine a sense of total ease and self-assurance, which comes with the habit of command, with a notorious jumpiness, a heightened sensitivity to slights and insults, the feeling that a man (and it is almost always a man) is somehow reduced, humiliated, if any 'debt of honor' is allowed to go unpaid."[90]

---

90   David Graeber, *Debt: The First 5,000 Years* (Brooklyn, NY: Melville House, 2011).

Does that sound like anyone you know? A surface demeanour of macho cool mixed with a deep, deep insecurity that leads to acts of cruelty and revenge? Does it sound like, I don't know, a few guys you know? Does it sound like, perhaps, a fair general assessment of the rotten core of contemporary masculinity? One where moments of male vulnerability—like injury, loss or emotional pain—are pathologized, minimized, hidden, ignored?

~

I was kind of annoying as a kid. I mean, annoyingness is in the eye (or the ear) of the beholder, but considering I probably had more enemies than friends in elementary school, it's fair to say that my personality grated on more than a handful of my classmates. I understood there was only so far I could go in terms of being snotty, but I still think back in wonderment, sometimes, that I was never the recipient of a schoolyard beatdown. For someone whose main weapon was my mouth, and who had no claims to any physical toughness, I must have presented an inviting target. Surely, at other, rougher elementary schools, I would have been toast. For my part, besides a few idle threats, the worst of my bullying was verbal.

Except for one incident.

One of the most damning things I know about masculinity is how different men's washrooms are from women's washrooms. They're both places for the disposal of bodily waste, for the functions of the body that we've agreed, societally, should be kept hidden. (More on this in Chapter 10.)

As such, public washrooms are necessarily places that are in danger of becoming disgusting more or less at the drop of a hat.

Most people do their best to clean up after themselves, but there are limits to how far they're willing to go, and it only takes one person stumbling out of a stall after having had explosive diarrhea, too faint to remember to flush, before the location is so haunted with odour and horror as to require a hazmat suit to enter. Without rigorous, regular cleaning on the part of people responsible for their maintenance, public washrooms are in permanent danger of deteriorating into hellholes.

But the tenor of washrooms that have been divided along sex or gender lines varies wildly in ways that are really fascinating.

For me, men's rooms have been spaces of discomfort for as long as I can remember.

I must not have been any older than ten. I wasn't talking to myself, singing, swaying. My pants weren't around my ankles. I was just standing at a urinal like any kid, my fly down, peeing, moving through the basic functions of the body.

There were two of them: a leader and a follower. A tale as old as time. I wasn't doing anything special. They came up right behind me—maybe one of them, maybe both, I don't remember. But one of them grabbed me by the shoulders and, with a gleefulness in his voice that is seared into my memory, started shaking me back and forth, yelling, "Don't piss on yourself! Don't piss on yourself!"

At the time it felt like bullying, maybe of a piece with certain forms of hazing, given that we were peers, it happened in private and involved the built-in logics of shame around genitals and bodily fluids that kids learn from a young age.

In retrospect, it was assault. Of course, the sheer physical violence of it was minimal. I don't even remember if I got any piss on myself, which is a good indicator that I probably didn't. The right move, tactically, would have been to shake me in a back-and-forth rocking motion, surely, rather than side-to-side. But it was calculated, not random; it was aggressive, it was designed to humiliate, to terrify, to debase.

Years later, I would wonder: What makes an 11-year-old assault someone if not a deep, intimate familiarity with how violence and fear work? What had this kid seen, what had he experienced, to get him to a point like that? In the words of the internet: "Who hurt you?" Of course, what experts call the cycle of abuse isn't a perfect circle. Being abused is no guarantee that you'll hurt others; hurting others is no guarantee that you were abused. But I don't believe boys get to a point like that of their own accord.

~

Why do men fight? Why are they violent? I'm not talking about boxing, or wrestling, or MMA fights. What I mean is, why do men hurt people? Why do they visit pain and suffering on others without warning, without consent?

Why are the people who commit violent assaults predominantly male, with men making up nearly 90% of homicide convictions in America in between 1980 and 2008,[91] and nearly 80% of aggravated assault arrests in 2011?[92] Why is contemporary masculinity so wrapped up in violence, in gun culture and anger? How do people who come out of the womb as babbling, helpless babies turn into killers in adolescence?

Much has been made, in the past few decades, about the impact of video games on young men's minds. It's not especially hard to see why: new technology is often made the scapegoat for cultural changes, regardless of its relationship to them. When people see the world changing in ways they don't understand, they look for easy answers. As school shootings punched through the haze of male anger into the mainstream, the problem of teen male violence could no longer be ignored. It didn't take critics long to finger violent video games as a likely suspect, especially when it came out that the perpetrators of the Columbine shooting played popular first-person shooters like *Doom* and *Quake*.

As I see it, video games probably have a small amount to do with rendering men increasingly comfortable with violence. But video games alone don't make killers and they never will. Rather, I believe boys who are already on path towards becoming violent will gravitate to violent

---

91   Cooper and Smith.
92   FBI, Crime in the United States 2011, table 66, https://ucr.fbi.gov/crime-in-the-u.s/2011/crime-in-the-u.s.-2011/tables/table_66_arrests_suburban_areas_by_sex_2011.xls.

video games because they reflect a pre-existing reality in that boy's head. Do they teach young men unrealistic things, do they help shape sexist attitudes, do they rob their users of time spent getting to know the real world? Absolutely. As Lundy Bancroft explores at length in *Why Does He Do That?*, male violence is ideological, not chemical or psychological: the men who commit intimate partner abuse aren't doing it because they're addicts or crazy people.[93] Rather, men are socialized to violence. The violent men are the ones who believe they are allowed to and justified in hurting women—the ones who buy in young to the story that causing pain is power.

The idea of superiority, of ownership over someone else, is a dangerous one. In the context of these abusive relationships, it leads to men treating their partners as property rather than as human beings. And when your property doesn't behave the way you want, it's only reasonable, they believe, to become frustrated, and to see it as defective, and then to lash out at it.

This mode—of violence, of domination, of conquering—is unhealthy, unnatural and deeply damaging both to young men and those around them. And, unfortunately, it represents the dominant strain of contemporary masculinity, online and off. In a powerful 2020 essay entitled "Bro Culture, Fitness, Chivalry, and American Identity," the writer Patrick Wyman explores this issue in depth.

---

93   Lundy Bancroft, *Why Does He Do That? Inside the Minds of Angry and Controlling Men* (New York: Penguin, 2003).

The code of American manhood that's developing out of this social-media melting pot has some aspects that bear watching: A love of firearms centered on tactical usefulness (for use in what context, exactly?), a vision of muscular physicality, self-defense as a personal obligation, an unquestioning hero-worship of military culture, and far too often, a deep suspicion of people who don't subscribe to this precise view of being a guy. Support the Troops, and if you don't, you're not really a man at all. If cops—quintessential subjects of Bro Culture—are told that they need to be bigger and stronger and quicker on the draw, that they're basically Troops, and that the targets of violence deserve what they get, what's the likely outcome of tense interactions between police and the people they're supposed to serve?

I'm deeply ambivalent about Bro Culture. Martial arts and fighting are enjoyable activities, but I have no illusions about what getting my ass kicked feels like. Lifting weights makes me feel good, but I'm never going to accomplish anything physical beyond what I can deadlift in my garage. I'm not bothered by firearms, though the tactical stuff seems absurd. I'm not averse to the general concept of being "gas-station-ready," to throw down if somebody threatens me at a convenience store, but I'm not sure that living life on constant edge in a world of perceived threats is healthy, realistic, or good for society. [94]

The upshot of this mentality that Wyman describes is you get a culture obsessed with testosterone, protein, weight-lifting beyond reason and crushing the weak. You get the increasing presence of muscle dysmorphia,[95] where men are literally unable to see the muscles they possess because they can never seem big or defined or impressive enough. You get a seemingly endless cycle of police killings in the news. You get families ripped apart by literal violence, but also bonds of love and trust eaten away by the acids of conspiracy theory, as men turn to prophets of hate who preach alpha dogma. You get a general climate of online discourse that feels more like a street fight than reasoned debate. Kill or be killed. Crush or be crushed.

~

It's a pretty common conception that at the root of every male confrontation is the possibility of physical violence. Whether it's road rage incidents, bar standoffs or "What the

94 Patrick Wyman, "Bro Culture, Fitness, Chivalry, and American Identity," *Perspectives: Past, Present, and Future*, December 3, 2020, https://patrickwyman.substack.com/p/bro-culture-fitness-chivalry-and.

95 Bethany Dawson, "Eating Disorders Are Stereotyped as Only Impacting Women and Girls. But Young Men Are Also Obsessing About Dieting and Appearance Leading to Muscle Dysmorphia," *Insider*, August 22, 2021, https://www.insider.com/muscle-dysmorphia-makes-me-feel-way-a-man-should-feel-2021-8.

fuck did you just say to my wife?" I believe most grown men have at some point found themselves in a situation that felt like a prelude to fisticuffs. And in an inherently violent dog-eat-dog world, there's a certain logic to that approach.

But, as Wyman notes, is that the world we really live in? How many of those tense situations actually evolve into a fight? And why should any of them? Not to sound like a grade school teacher, but physical fighting literally doesn't solve anything—it just leaves people angry and bruised, or worse.

And while bruises fade over time, the emotional scars can live on. Guys often don't realize how much violence cheapens the world they live in. Perhaps the biggest upshot is how little men are trusted, how often people assume the worst about them and their behaviour.

bell hooks understood this problem all too well. In *The Will to Change*, she writes, "This fear of maleness that they inspire estranges men from every female in their lives to greater or lesser degrees, and men feel the loss."

"Ultimately, one of the emotional costs of allegiance to patriarchy is to be seen as unworthy of trust," she continues. "If women and girls in patriarchal culture are taught to see every male, including the males with whom we are intimate, as potential rapists and murderers, then we cannot offer them our trust, and without trust there is no love."[96]

I think about this whenever I think about the relationship between men and children. How often it seems like

---

96   hooks, *The Will to Change*.

they're assumed to be pedophiles or would-be kidnappers if they pay even a little bit of attention to kids who aren't their own. What kind of a society have we constructed where half the adult population is considered suspect for wanting to interact with any of the child population unless they're blood relatives? Collectively, men have, through their violence and their harm, lost our trust. And their worlds are smaller for it.

What can you do to start re-earning that trust? What I mean when I say "walk away from a fight" is to start thinking about engaging in conflict—whether it's digital, verbal or physical—as losing a fight in and of itself. When you enter into a fight, whether it's a fistfight, a shoving match or just a dick-measuring contest, you're losing the struggle to be a complex, thoughtful, rational individual and giving over, not to your baser instincts, but to lessons you've been taught about power and masculinity. It's time for men to start thinking about approaches other than fighting. What does conflict resolution look like? What does apology or forgiveness look like? What does saying, "Hey, agree to disagree" look like?

A world where men see violence as a last resort, rather than their only tool, where they see aggression and conflict as things to de-escalate and reject, would be a world where a lot of the hurt and fear we take for granted today would not exist. Getting there will require widespread recognition that contemporary masculinity's love affair with violence and machismo isn't a reflection of timeless, eternal manhood but of a specific cultural moment. It'll require men, as individuals and as a collective, to reorient what being strong means, what losing a fight means, what honour means. It'll require instances where taunts are not returned, where people are called pussies and just let it slide, where what angry men have termed cowardice starts to be recognized as rationality. It'll require the telling—and re-telling—of new kinds of stories.

9

break the bro code

"The bond between two men is stronger than the bond
between a man and a woman because, on average,
men are stronger than women. That's just science."

—Barney Stinson and Matt Kuhn, *The Playbook*

The bro code as it exists today has many different
manifestations. To a degree, it already feels like a
bit of an anachronism, something whose heyday in North
American culture was the late 2000s into the early 2010s,
maybe—hence the epigraph for this chapter, from a book
published in 2008, "co-written" by a fictional character
of a TV show that premiered in 2005.

But though the phrase itself may have fallen out of
favour a little bit, the mentality it exemplifies is far from
gone, and, like any lumbering behemoth past its prime,
is still able to cause incredible harm.

Close your eyes and imagine. Bro code culture is a
sound: loud frat boys bragging about their sexual conquests.
A smell: cheap cologne hiding body odour, maybe Axe

deodorant. Bro code culture is a taste: low-quality vodka mixed with vomit. Bro code culture is a physical sensation: hands on your chest, shoving you. Asking you if you want to go. Asking if you want to go, *right now*.

But all that posturing, all those signifiers, aren't what's especially toxic about bro code culture. They're bro-ey, yes, and cringe, but they're not codified. Women can act like bros, too, and bros, regardless of gender, can be ultimately harmless. So often bro culture is just empty posturing for a young man still trying to figure himself out, as young men have always had to. What's harmful about bro culture is the hardening of these attributes into an idea, an ethos, a code, one that's distributed along strict lines—and enforced. What's toxic about the bro code is a shared understanding that any and all masculine behaviour is worth valorizing while any and all feminine behaviour is worth denigrating. That any and all male speech is worth repeating, and all female speech is worth shouting over. That any and all men are worth protecting, and all women are worth throwing under the bus.

And when enough people believe this kind of stuff and start acting in concert with each other, you get unbelievably bad outcomes. You get men hurting and harming the women around them and getting away with it. You get men behaving irresponsibly, dangerously, violently and being praised for it. You get men whose seeming only politics is to uphold other men who think, look, talk and act like them.

The bro code, functionally, works much the same way any system of cruelty and inequality works. It works by allowing a certain group of people to deny full personhood to anyone outside their circle, to shortcut around being a caring, empathetic human being. It works by making a group of people feel strong as they band together. But once they've banded together, it gives them license—and in fact, a desire—to be cruel to others.

So, you get the old boys' club. Business deals done on the golf course. Promotions handed out to the up-and-coming hot-shot without a thought for seniority or fit or, often, merit. Logically and morally incoherent online articles that claim that "a bro is never allowed to drive in a drunken state. An exception can be made in the case of a bro who has acquired masters in the art of drunken driving."[97] You get spaces that are blander, poorer, emptier for the lack of gender diversity. And, surprising no one, when groups are formed without a thought to gender diversity—or, rather, in the spirit of erasing it—other forms of diversity tend not to flourish. In short, bro culture is a monoculture—an exaltation of one kind of masculinity, into whose narrow outline many men try to fit themselves to their own detriment.

~

But what is the bro code, exactly? How does it function? Why does it exist?

---

97   Ankush Bahuguna, "All You Need to Know About the Bro-Code," MensXP, October 14, 2020, https://www.mensxp.com/relationships/friendship/21638-all-you-need-to-know-about-the-brocode.html.

In a 2020 article for *Ms.* magazine called "Bad Cops and Bystanders: How Male-Dominated Cultures Keep Men Silent," written in the wake of the murder of George Floyd, Jackson Katz, a filmmaker and author, describes the role that a bro-code-like ethos plays in many all-male groups and organizations: "Whether it's called a boy code, a guy code, or a bro code, a set of unwritten rules governs the behavior of individuals in all-male or male-dominated groups. This is especially true of groups engaged in aggressive competition and 'us versus them' battles with other groups—such as in sports and politics, and is even more pronounced in military or para-military organizations such as the police."[98]

Guys who buy into bro culture, withstanding the hazing and cruelty that are often required to access it, according to sociologist Michael Kimmel in the 2015 documentary *The Mask You Live In*, get two things: They get, as they see it, "the bonds that are the most impermeable, the ones that will last you a lifetime." And, he adds, they "also get the feeling that, 'Girls can't do this.' So you get both horizontal solidarity with your bros, and hierarchy: 'Men are superior to women.'"[99]

If you read up on the bro code in books or in online articles you're served with a variety of different messages

98   Jackson Katz, "Bad Cops and Bystanders: How Male-Dominated Cultures Keep Men Silent," *Ms.*, June 17, 2020, https://msmagazine.com/2020/06/17/george-floyd-bad-cops-and-bystanders-how-male-dominated-cultures-keep-men-silent/. First encountered in Sonora Jha, *How to Raise a Feminist Son.*
99   The Representation Project, https://therepproject.org/films/the-mask-you-live-in/. First encountered in Lewis Howes, *The Mask of Masculinity* (New York: Rodale, 2019).

about what it actually constitutes. Sometimes it forbids hitting on a bro's sister, girlfriend or ex; other times, there are loopholes. Sometimes it's about helping your bros get laid; other times, it's about ensuring they don't get in trouble when they cross a line. Of course, any time one person sets out to write down what the bro code they swear by means, they're leaving out another person's version. But whatever the surface details, the core remains similar: loyalty to the bros.

As Kimmel puts it: "The most important dicta of the bro code is you never rat out the brotherhood. You never, ever betray that brotherhood. So this leads to the notion that surrounding bad things, there's a code of silence. What happens is their heads and their hearts actually come into conflict. Because their hearts may be saying, 'This is wrong. I know this is wrong. My ethical compass tells me this is wrong. I should do something about it. A man would act.' And on the other hand: 'But these are my bros. I can't betray them. If I do, they'll marginalize me.' This is the fear that so many men have that keeps them from acting ethically."

Moments later in the documentary, the author Tony Porter frames it this way: "There's a choice. And many times the choice is rooted in our privilege. So while we as 'good men' don't perpetrate the violence, we are part of the collective socialization, the fertile ground that's required for the violence to exist."

Without guys who shut up and provide that tacit support for the guys who are acting badly, there is no bro culture. If the heavy silence at the bottom dissolves, the whole pyramid crumbles. There's a reason you see this in bro culture and not in more gender-diverse friend groups.

"Diversity" is more than a PC buzzword. It's important because, as I'll explore in more depth in Chapter 12, groups, organizations and cultures made up of only one kind of person are vulnerable. They're prone to engaging in groupthink, struggling to solve problems obvious to other, more diverse groups, where different backgrounds and skill sets can tackle a variety of issues. Groups of historians where everyone is straight struggle to recognize when someone they're studying was clearly in a gay relationship; groups of archeologists where everyone is a man struggle to recognize when tools they've unearthed were clearly used by women.

Groups where everyone is a guy socialized to respect power and masculinity and to stay silent—in other words, groups in the thrall of the bro code—have their own weaknesses. While the bro code may be intended to protect guys at the expense of their female peers, sanctifying and covering up everything from mistreatment, emotional cruelty and sexism to sexual assault, harassment and rape, it's not too hard to see it at work in scandal after scandal in male-dominated environments—university football programs, junior hockey championship teams, police departments. The cases that make the headlines are an outcrop, the top of the pyramid of a system where harm to anyone outside your bubble is considered unimportant compared to the harm of someone within your bubble facing justified and proportionate repercussions for committing that harm. This is the logical conclusion of bro culture, no matter how sick and horrifying it would be to most bros. If you build social structures around protecting one kind of person at the expense of everyone else, don't be surprised when they work exactly as intended.

~

As for me, I can't say I have a lot of first-hand experience with the bro code, as such.

It's, after all, hard to be party to the bro code when you're not generally seen as a bro. I feel like I can count on one hand the number of times guys I know have taken me into their confidence to divulge things they would never tell a woman. If such a thing exists, I feel like I'm probably more familiar with the anti–bro code. So many of my female friends have opened up to me about things they'd be hesitant to tell lots of guys—stories of male violence, cruelty or mistreatment, mostly—that those are the ones I can no longer count.

In university, my program, creative writing, comprised mostly female students, and the place where I spent most of my extra-curricular time, the college newspaper, was, for the many years I spent there, almost always hovering around gender parity. I didn't seek out male-dominated spaces, and no one drew me into them. If not for what I've heard from friends of mine, and what I've seen in the culture generally, I might only dimly know such a thing as the bro code existed.

But I did see it in action when I was in university—in a way. Though we might associate the phrase more with frat bros aged 18 to 21, the same mentality can play out with older guys, particularly if they're not much interested in growing up. That's what a few of the teachers who taught my undergraduate creative writing classes were like—a group of male friends who drank a lot and used their status to woo young women in their late teens and early 20s. Though there was nothing against teacher-student relationships in the university handbook at the time, this group of men took advantage of young and ambitious female writers, pursuing new ones as each year brought a fresh crop of impressionable and starstruck undergrads to their courses. In their mid-30s and 40s, they watched each other date teenagers and 20-year-olds—young women who were trying to make a place for themselves in a field where these men had established careers—and kept each other's secrets.

This culture pervaded the program and was an open secret for years. Though various people tried to address it in different ways, nothing seemed to change until one of the men finally came forward with an open letter posted online. National scandal followed, and the remaining teachers were shuffled out of their jobs by the university. I'm sure dating young women they had power over was a lot of fun for them in the moment. But what they were doing was wrong, and at times involved alleged sexual assault. It was never healthy, and it was never something to be proud of. If they knew that this was how it was going to end—their writing careers functionally over, their jobs gone, their friends and acquaintances having cut ties—would they have still gone about it the same way?

Of course, men don't have exclusive rights to the bro-code mentality. In Sarah Schulman's landmark 2016 book, *Conflict Is Not Abuse*, she explores the ways that, as the title suggests, conflict can feel like abuse to some people—people who are either not used to being challenged or who have trauma from past instances of abuse. In some cases, this plays out in marginalized people overreacting to feelings of discomfort or hurt; in others, it plays out in members of a dominant culture doing just the same.[100] In this way, the circle-the-wagons precepts of the bro code can be embodied by people of any gender, and as women gain social power in certain spheres, their ability to use tactics like this to harm others will increase. Ultimately, what can be toxic about certain iterations of so-called woke cancel culture is also what's toxic about bro code culture. It's privileging someone's identity over their actual personhood, it's making important, damning, harmful, difficult decisions according to the simple rubric of whether someone falls inside a group or outside it, it's consigning someone to non-entity because it's easier to do that than to reckon with the complexity of human interaction in its fullness.

~

If you do any digging, the statistics about sexual assault in college, or just in life generally, are staggering. It's more

100   Sarah Schulman, *Conflict Is Not Abuse: Overstating Harm, Community Responsibility, and the Duty of Repair* (Vancouver: Arsenal Pulp, 2016).

common than you think, reported less often than you think, falsely accused much less often than you think and more damaging to the victims' lives than you think.[101] I say this as someone who gleefully claimed that I'd "raped that test" more than once in high school. At the time, my friends and I understood it as akin to saying you'd killed something. When you say, "Yo, bro, you killed that," people tend not to get angry on behalf of murder victims. And at the time, I didn't know any rape victims—although, looking back, statistically, I must have known at least a few. But the prevalence of rape, and the seriousness of it, wasn't remotely obvious to me as a teen, as it isn't to many teen boys, even in our post-#MeToo society.

That, perhaps, is the worst thing about bro culture—that it's constituted primarily of people who have little to no direct understanding of rape or consent, who stand to benefit the most and suffer the least from the sort of black box our society puts sexual consent into, and who possess a willful unwillingness to learn. That's not to say that every teen boy or young man is like this; rather, it's to say that far too many are, some egregiously, and of the ones who aren't, more of them seem to prefer neutrality than outright opposition. And as the late Archbishop Desmond Tutu famously said, "If you are neutral in situations of injustice, you have chosen the side of the oppressor."

---

101   Resilience. "Sexual Violence Myths and Facts," https://www.ourresilience.org/what-you-need-to-know/myths-and-facts/; Rape Crisis, England and Wales, "Myths vs Facts," https://rapecrisis.org.uk/get-informed/about-sexual-violence/myths-vs-realities/.

Of course, the second, less-shared part of that quote is "If an elephant has its foot on the tail of a mouse and you say that you are neutral, the mouse will not appreciate your neutrality." I think part of the problem is, for lots of guys, an unwillingness to see the situation framed in those terms. How are men the elephant and women the mouse? That may have been a clear-cut truth in the 18th century, but in the 2020s, it's not so obvious. Women can vote, inherit property, run for office and, as I'll address at length in Chapter 13, are closing the academic and economic gaps on men with startling speed. Increasingly, it doesn't make sense to frame the problem as exclusively gender-based. According to data from the U.S. Department of Labor, the median annual earnings for white and Asian women in America is much higher than that of Black and Hispanic men, for instance.[102] Certainly, these women are incarcerated and policed at much lower rates.[103] To talk about power and privilege without acknowledging facts like these is a kind of tunnel vision, one that many feminists still engage in, unfortunately.

But these facts don't change the reality that rape, assault and harassment are still, overwhelmingly, things committed by men and experienced by women. Yes, there are male victims; yes, there are female perpetrators. But sexual violence is a masculinity problem, and in colleges and universities, women are overwhelmingly the ones bearing

---

102   U.S. Department of Labor, "Median Annual Earnings by Sex, Race and Hispanic Ethnicity," https://www.dol.gov/agencies/wb/data/earnings/median-annual-sex-race-hispanic-ethnicity.
103   National Institute of Justice, "Figure 2. U.S. Incarceration Rates by Race and Sex," https://nij.ojp.gov/media/image/19511.

the brunt. I bring this up because perhaps the most critical function of bro culture is shielding men from the consequences of engaging in this exact kind of behaviour.

Young men's willingness to engage in it, of course, is not some about-face. It's a logical continuation from behaviours inculcated in them as boys—that masculinity is a kind of code and that, as such, adherence to it sometimes requires difficult decisions, decisions that fly in the face of kindergarten-level morality. In *Raising Cain*, Kindlon and Thompson write of the losses boys go through as they shift into their teen years and childhood gives way to adolescence.

> Throughout these losses—of friendship, of trust, and of self-esteem—and the emotional shutdown required to achieve the Big Impossible of manhood, the culture of cruelty imposes a code of silence on boys, requiring them to suffer without speaking of it and to be silent witnesses to acts of cruelty to others. The power of this code is so strong, and it is such a pervasive part of the masculine identity, that boys take it for granted. They keep quiet for a variety of reasons. They fear being victimized again. They don't want to be responsible for disciplinary actions against other boys. They don't want to be ostracized from the peer group. They have learned their lessons well. To remain silent is strong and masculine, and to speak out is not.[104]

---

104 Kindlon and Thompson.

Let's return to Jackson Katz, who I quoted earlier. The above plays neatly into some of the things he explores in the 2018 documentary *The Bystander Moment*. As he puts it, "If you're a man, and you're in a position to challenge and interrupt other men's sexism, but you choose to remain silent, then in a sense your silence is a form of consent and complicity in those men's sexism."[105]

Of course it makes sense for young men to abide by the bro code as they watch, or hear, or simply learn about their fellow bros engaging in horrible acts. They're scared. And it's easier to stay silent, a kind of inertia, than to speak up, to set off a chain reaction of responses. Who knows where it might lead?

~

Like I said early, women have experienced a ton of sexual assault. If women you know haven't told you about it, it's not because it's not happening—it's because they don't trust you.

But men also experience sexual assault. More than you realize. These things are impossible to track with 100% accuracy, but the CDC suggests that, for American men, it's nearly one in four.[106] One in four. You definitely know more than four guys. You probably know hundreds of guys.

---

105   The Media Education Foundation, *The Bystander Moment*, directed by Jeremy Earp (2018), http://bystandermoment.org/.
106   Centers for Disease Control and Prevention, "Intimate Partner Violence, Sexual Violence, and Stalking Among Men," https://www.cdc.gov/violenceprevention/intimatepartnerviolence/men-ipvsvandstalking.html.

But regardless of whether you're one of the lucky ones who's never been a victim of a sexual assault, there's a good chance you haven't heard that kind of thing from a number of your friends, relatives or acquaintances. There's a good chance you haven't heard that kind of thing from a single guy.

And the deafening silence around it, the reason you're not hearing about it? It's for the same reason women don't tell the men they know. If the men in a man's life haven't told him about their experiences with sexual assault, it's because they don't trust him, either.

When it comes to this kind of admission, men might even have a higher threshold for trusting each other than women do for trusting men. They fear a loss of status that women can't necessarily claim to have in the first place. To admit to being a victim—in lots of ways, but in this way particularly—is anathema to far too many guys' core concepts of what it is to be a man.

But when your conception of what a man is elides the all-too-real, horrible lived experiences of one in four men right off the bat, then your conception of what a man is is horribly flawed.

That kind of logic runs through all kinds of aspects of male friendship, sadly. If there's going to be anything like a code of brotherhood, of trust and genuine fraternity between men, it can't be, "I will protect you when a woman you've hurt comes knocking." It has to be, "I will protect you when you are hurting." The first code is a flimsy thing, harmful to everyone involved, structurally useful only to propagate harm for the short-term pleasure of a few. The second code is real manhood, in the sense that being a man means being an adult just as much as it means being male.[107]

The first code, the unhealthy bro groupthink, relies as much on the silence of participants as it does on their agreement. It's not a code that calls upon you to act so much as it's a code that calls upon you to stifle your instinct to do something in certain specific situations.

But, as Lundy Bancroft explains in *Why Does He Do That?*, individual men have more power to shift momentum than they realize—whether in a single conversation, in a group or in a community.

"If you are a man, your refusal to fall in step with destructive jokes and comments can be especially powerful," he writes. "Men have a particularly important role to play in cultural change. When a father tells his son, 'I don't want to hear you saying bad things about girls' . . . the boy sits up and takes notice."[108] Similarly, all it takes is one guy speaking up to immediately change the conversation—and with attitudes on sexual assault changing in recent years, one guy is likely to be supported by others.

In a 2017 article I edited for AskMen called "What to Do When Your Friend Gets Called Out," Kitty Stryker

---

107   That's something we forget sometimes. I read somewhere—I can't seem to find the source of the quote—that when Americans want to insult a man, they call him a woman, but when Europeans want to insult a man, they call him a boy. Of course, this is an oversimplification, but regardless of the actual habits of Americans, Europeans or anyone else, it invokes an interesting idea—the question of what failing to be a man means about you, and how likely that is to change over time.

108   Bancroft.

explains that "sexual abusers tend to surround themselves with people who will apologize for them, who will cover for them, who will defend them. They require camouflage in the form of a group of people who will confirm that the abuser is 'such a nice guy.' It's how they can repeatedly get away with violating boundaries and how they can escape being outed or banished. It's how they ensure their victims won't be believed."[109]

So when I say "break the bro code," what I mean is, don't be one of those guys covering for an abuser. Value doing the right thing over how you're perceived. Value sticking to your guns and acting according to your principles over trying to maintain status with a clique of guys whose approval you crave. Value others—regardless of their gender, their race, their ethnicity, their sexual orientation—not because they belong to the right in-crowd, but because of who they are as people, how they treat you and how they treat everyone else.

Your life is richer when your friendships are a diverse ecosystem and not a monoculture, and society is better off when groups aren't segregated from one another, when it's a beautiful mixture, not a collection of constrained, straitjacketed cliques, slowly driven crazy by the reinforcing feedback loops of the lies they tell themselves about everyone else.

109   Kitty Stryker, "What To Do When Your Friend Gets Called Out," AskMen, https://www.askmen.com/dating/dating_advice/what-to-do-when-your-friend-gets-called-out.html.

10

~~the least manly thing you can do is~~
play with your own butthole

"If the phallus is essentially social, the anus is essentially private."

—Guy Hocquenghem, *Homosexual Desire*

For many people, hearing that a guy enjoys anal pleasure—whether that's having his butthole tongued, fingered, penetrated by sex toys and/or penises—is grounds to call the guy gay or, at the very least, not straight. What straight man would possibly enjoy having his anus played with? It doesn't even need to be a regular thing. For certain orthodox devotees of heterosexuality, a guy trying it one time is grounds for stripping him of his straight card.

I've seen a fair amount of pushback to that mentality from people who see this as reductive and demeaning and homophobic, who say a guy putting something up his butt—or getting someone else to do just that—isn't gay unless he's fantasizing about another guy while it happens. But I'm of the mindset that it's a logically sound argument. People aren't wrong when they say it's a little bit gay for a guy to enjoy anal pleasure. If you take it at its word, straight, cisgender masculinity is about penetrating, controlling and dominating women. It has no room in its playbook for relaxing, lying back and letting yourself be penetrated, regardless of who's doing the penetration.

Where I disagree with people who say this is simply on the question of whether or not being a little bit gay is a bad thing. As you may have been able to surmise by this point in the book, I don't believe there's any amount of gay that should be considered bad, just as there's no amount of straight (or anything in between) that should be considered bad either. Sexual attraction is a spectrum, and to whatever degree Western society understands that today, cultures throughout history have recognized it to varying degrees. The remaining vestiges of homophobia that constitute North America's contemporary stance on sexuality are an incredibly small-minded approach to something vast and beautiful and complex.

But you probably know all that already, so I won't waste too much more ink on it. What I want to evangelize for in this chapter isn't being gay, per se, it's being brave enough to explore, understand and experiment with your own body. Which, in this particular way, is a little bit gay.

~

There's a decent chance you've never engaged in any kind of anal sex—surveys suggest only a minority of men have. But if porn aggregator sites are anything to go off, these days, anal sex is incredibly normal—conceptually uncontroversial, if not common in real life. If you go back to even the early 2010s, however, anal sex was still pretty taboo, considered a sort of underground sex act, something more shameful and dirtier than so-called regular vaginal penetration. The prior decade was more of the same. An infamous 2004 article in *XXL* mag asked 27 famous rappers their thoughts on anal sex, and, though most rappers aren't ones to pass up an opportunity to brag about their sexual prowess, all but a handful of them said, essentially, "No thank you," with many claiming it was a disgusting concept altogether. [110]

But while anal might be a relatively recent entrant into mainstream—read: straight—sexuality, putting things into the human asshole is hardly something new. Anal sex, as a practice, is one that goes back thousands of years of recorded history, and likely many more unrecorded. Today, it's perhaps most famously associated with the culture of ancient Greece, but it's been documented in many different parts of the globe. Not only that, anal activity has been recorded in many different corners of the animal kingdom, from primates to dolphins to sheep to polecats to giraffes, and its practitioners are quite often two males going at it, to say nothing of at least one photo I came across as a teen of an MMF threesome daisy-chaining penetration between two stags and a doe.

In short, the pleasure possibilities held within the anus are ones that diverse beings throughout the planet's history have figured out of their own accord, without

---

110   *XXL Magazine*, July 2004.

access to modern products like silicone-based lube or poppers, and without coded references in pop songs or scandalized discussion on HBO sitcoms. In many cases, they did so without even having hands to guide the penis into the anus.

Why does anal feel good, exactly? Well, if you speak to people on the receiving end, much of the time, it doesn't especially. It doesn't unless there's a good amount of lube, and unless the lube's slipperiness holds up as long as the penetration does. It doesn't if the penetrating object is too big, or the anus being penetrated is too tight. It doesn't if the person being penetrated is feeling tense and uncomfortable or if they're having digestive issues. There are a lot of reasons it might not—but most of those reasons also apply to vaginal penetration. And that doesn't mean there isn't enormous pleasure potential therein, when handled the right way, and it doesn't mean that so many straight men's genuine fear of their own assholes is remotely warranted.

Because, after all, the human anus is a site of incredible sensitivity. Even better, because it's located in close proximity to the genitals, anal penetration can cause stimulation of the incredibly sensitive prostate in people assigned male at birth and can also stimulate portions of the clitero-urethral-vaginal complex for people assigned female at birth.

Regardless of sex or gender, most people can't orgasm from anal penetration alone, but most cis women can't orgasm from vaginal penetration alone either, and many of them still engage in a great deal of it. Put simply, in the right conditions, anal penetration can feel incredibly nice. And so few straight guys are aware of that, let alone willing to consider trying it out.

Part of the problem is poor sex education, of course. As Jonathan Zimmerman describes in his book *Too Hot to Handle: A Global History of Sex Education*, attempts to push for almost any form of sex education have met with enormous resistance in essentially every country of the world for over a century now.[111] If the issue of even teaching young people the most basic biological truths about their bodies and those of their peers is still a controversial concept, the idea of exploring the human anus as a site of pleasure, not just an organ for defecation, seems unbelievably improbable and remote.

~

I get it. I'm no stranger to discomfort around my body, shame about my so-called private parts or learning far too late the proper way to clean myself. As I mentioned in Chapter 5, I experienced a foreskin condition called phimosis growing up, and wasn't aware it wasn't standard until around age 19. When I watched porn as a teenager and saw the penis heads of the actors out in the open, not covered in foreskin, I simply assumed all porn stars were circumcised. Of course it makes sense to me that lots of guys are operating more or less in the dark when it comes to their so-called private parts—I was too.

---

111   Jonathan Zimmerman, *Too Hot to Handle: A Global History of Sex Education* (Princeton: Princeton University Press, 2015).

Moreover, it wasn't until my mid-20s that I learned that standing up to wipe after pooping was considered non-standard or even that anyone stayed sitting down to wipe. Growing up, no one talks about these things, and if anyone does, they'd be considered intensely weird. It honestly feels like many guys are afraid to acknowledge that they even poop at all, let alone that it has occurred or will occur in any specific circumstances.

Of course, there's nothing especially ridiculous about the seemingly particularly male discomfort around the anus. The French philosopher Guy Hocquenghem, analyzing the work of his compatriots Gilles Deleuze and Félix Guattari, explores the matter in depth in a 1972 essay called "Family, Capitalism, Anus," going so far as to claim that, because people who can't control their defecation, like babies and the very elderly, require care from other people, "knowing how to 'hold it in' or, on the contrary, when to release one's excrement, is indispensable to the proper formation of the self." [112] In no small part because of their power to, if ingested, cause illness, feces are deeply taboo in essentially every culture and have been, seemingly, since time immemorial. So, because of the power your excrement has to ruin your social standing—just try being popular in school after shitting your pants, or merely being the subject of pants-shitting rumours—the anus is a site of incredible danger, a thing that must be mastered.

112   Guy Hocquenghem, "Family, Capitalism, Anus," in *Homosexual Desire*, 2nd ed., trans. Daniella Dangoor (London: Allison & Busby, 1978).

To some degree, we all do this: as kids, we learn to hold it in until we're over the toilet, learn to hide the material, the sounds, the smells that the anus can produce as best we can. But there's a lingering tension around this contract, one that young boys understand all too well. So many of the jokes and gross-out songs I learned in the school-yard as a kid had some kind of scatological element to them. Even saying the word "poop" at the right moment could probably reduce a classroom of eight-year-olds to hysterical laughter. But comedy is a roadmap to fear. We joke about things that make us uncomfortable, to reclaim control over them.

Many guys, as boys and young men, deal with this tension, and the fear of the power their anus holds, not by becoming masters of their own anuses, not by knowing them inside and out, but by trying to ignore the hole as best they can. It's no surprise that we encounter articles like *MEL* magazine's "What It's Like to Be a Guy Who Doesn't Clean His Ass," detailing Reddit threads where men ask for anonymous online help with the unpleasant reality of poop stains—or, just as often, women asking on behalf of their male partners who won't address the issue.[113]

Because the truth about many guys' senses of discomfort around their anuses is that it extends well beyond the bedroom. You only need to read so many accounts of adult men who don't know how to properly clean their buttholes

---

113   Quinn Myers, "What It's Like to Be a Guy Who Doesn't Clean His Ass," *MEL*, https://melmagazine.com/en-us/story/what-its-like-to-be-a-guy-who-doesnt-clean-his-ass.

before you start to feel concerned.[114] How, exactly, does this happen? Like many issues surrounding masculinity, it feels multipronged: men aren't taught how to do something by those most responsible, but are taught to feel shame about the issue, are also taught not to ask for help with things, and so just blunder through their lives with no real idea of what's going on.

Step one in this failure, is, of course, the parents or parent figures not passing this kind of information along properly. Contemporary Western culture is one where there are significant gaps in the male knowledge that's passed down from generation to generation. Stereotypically, fathers love to teach their sons how to play team sports, or other appropriately masculine skills like driving, or maybe fixing certain things, perhaps barbecuing. What they rarely do is teach their sons about their bodies—especially their private parts.

It's not about the anus, but let's look at bell hooks describing parents talking to their sons about their penises in her 2004 book, *The Will to Change*, for a glimpse of the dynamic at play here:

> Little boys learn early in life that . . . sexual desire should not be freely expressed and that females will try to control male sexuality. For boys this issue of control begins with the mother's

---

114 Something worth considering: North America is slow on the uptake here, but many other parts of the world prioritize bidet use over toilet paper, and these days, bidet attachments are increasingly easy to come by. In my experience, it really is a better way to live.

response to his penis; usually she does not like it and she does not know what to do with it. Her discomfort with his penis communicates that there is something inherently wrong with it. She does not communicate to the boy child that his penis is wonderful, special, marvelous. This same fear of the boy's penis is commonly expressed by fathers who simply do not concern themselves with educating boys about their bodies. Sadly, unenlightened approaches to child abuse lead many parents to fear celebration of their child's body, especially the boy body, which may respond to playful physical closeness with an erection. In patriarchal culture everyone is encouraged to see the penis, even the penis of a small boy, as a potential weapon. This is the psychology of a rape culture. Boys learn that they should identify with the penis and the potential pleasure erections will bring, while simultaneously learning to fear the penis as though it were a weapon that could backfire, rendering them powerless, destroying them. Hence the underlying message boys receive about sexual acts is that they will be destroyed if they are not in control, exercising power.[115]

That dynamic—of fear and discomfort leading to silence, of silence combined with masculine ideology leading to unhealthy lessons—is similar to the one we see with the

---

115   hooks, *The Will to Change*.

anus. Past a certain age, being too physically close to your son, talking to him about his body and his relationship to it, starts to feel taboo. Parents withdraw. Faced with silence, the kid is left to figure things out for himself. This isn't a uniquely male problem; there's a good chance you've encountered a story where a young girl, experiencing menstruation for the first time, thinks there's something horribly wrong with her and feels compelled to hide it from everyone, including her parents—but it is something that is worsened by the male attitude towards penetration itself, which is entwined with how men are taught to see gay men, and how men are taught to see women.

~

Ultimately, at the heart of the male discomfort around the anus is a desire not to be female. Growing up, boys learn that being a man is good and being a woman is bad. *You throw like a girl. Don't be a sissy. Man up.* Then they learn that sex is a process of men putting their penises into women. It doesn't take a genius to figure out that boys of 10 and 12 start thinking: *For everything to go according to plan, I must only penetrate. If I'm penetrated, then I'm a woman, and that's bad.* It's only a few leaps of logic away for men who prefer to penetrate men to be equally tarnished. At the root of contemporary homophobia is the deep, deep misogyny that runs through our culture.

Apart from the inherent tragedies of those ideologies of hatred, it's also too bad because, although homophobes would have you believe otherwise, historically, many cultures throughout the world have historically seen nothing wrong with men making love to other men, in some cases constructing it as an inherently masculine trait.

It's also illogical for people to assume sexual orientation is inherently bound up in gender. It seems like a mistake that Western culture has been making for as long as sexual orientation has been a topic of discussion. The concept of gaydar, for instance, has much more to do with gender presentation than it does with desire or attraction— according to the logic of gaydar, you don't spot a gay guy by looking at who he kisses, but at how he dresses, how he speaks. But a simple look at actual gay men gives the lie to this logic; I've known both incredibly, annoyingly macho gay guys and plenty of effete, tender straight men.

Still, the aversion so many adult men feel towards homosexuality in the abstract and gay men in the concrete starts to take shape when they're still young, thrust forward, in some cases, by some of the same schoolyard tension around the scatological that I described earlier in this chapter. You encounter scenes like this one from Kindlon and Thompson's *Raising Cain*:

> Tom, the new kid at school—a boy who also happened to have long blond hair and feminine features—upped the fear level of other boys in the ninth-grade class. One, a boy named Greg, was accused of being attracted to Tom. Greg's tormentors chalked the boys' names together in a heart on the school's front sidewalk and whispered "faggot" whenever they passed him in the

halls. One day they put a stick of butter in Greg's locker—butter being the preferred lubricant for anal intercourse in their worldview—and from that point on, they would just walk by him and whisper "butter." The ringleaders of this harassment were boys who were experimenting sexually themselves, engaging in group mutual masturbation activities. Their harassment of Greg was an effort to vigorously defend themselves against their own homosexual panic and the fact that they even noticed that the new boy was attractive—and what did that suggest about *them*?[116]

A disdain for women bleeds into disdain for gay men, which leads to a fear of being penetrated, and thus, a fear of the anus entirely. By the same token, respect for women leads to acceptance of gay men, which leads to the fear falling away. Once you realize that, it's a whole new ballgame.

~

My first time was in the shower. I used my pinky finger—what else? I wanted the smallest thing I had complete control over, the smallest thing I knew for sure wouldn't get stuck. Using a foreign object, besides the danger of my sphincter pulling it into my ass and requiring a hospital visit, also meant I'd forever have to look at it and see it as

---

116 Kindlon and Thompson.

"the thing I put up my ass that one time." With a finger, it's different. You already have a pre-established relationship. There's no danger of permanently recontextualizing your finger.

In any case, that first time—I must have been in my late teens or early 20s—not a lot happened on a physical level. I didn't have an experience of blissful anal pleasure. I didn't convulse with orgasm. I didn't instantly become addicted to the sensation of being penetrated.

But the not-a-lot-happening aspect of it was also instructive. Because other things didn't happen: I didn't experience pain. I didn't experience revulsion. I didn't come out of it feeling tainted, ruined or in any way more or less attracted to men. (And, perhaps most importantly for my younger self's understanding of the anus, I didn't find a dark brown smear on my finger.)

Instead, I had a private physical experience. I learned something about my body, and I busted a few myths. It didn't make me a little bit gay—what made me a little bit gay was fantasizing about giving a blowjob to a sexy hockey player who played for my favourite team.

I had a not terribly dissimilar experience a few years later with an ex-partner of mine. We'd explored anilingus a little—I was going down on them—when they suggested we try the inverse. It hadn't occurred to me, but I wasn't opposed to the idea. We gave it a shot. I didn't hate the experience. It wasn't something I had any special desire to do again, but I was glad I'd agreed to it. I learned something about my preferences, and I could now say with a straight face that I'd had my asshole licked in bed, and it was fine—a little tickly for my tastes, but I could see how other people would really enjoy it.

When it comes to penetrative anal play, there's really only a handful of rules. Don't insert any object unless it was designed for that purpose. Not because it's immoral or whatever, but because without a flared base, your ass muscles will pull things up inside you, and then you have to visit the emergency room to get a carrot, or a remote control, or a beer bottle, or whatever you had lying around removed from your own anus. Stick with sex toys—butt plugs, anal beads and so forth—or with body parts, like I did. If you're using anything bigger than a finger—and even then, it's not a bad idea—use lube. In a pinch, spit will do, but if you're trying to genuinely enjoy yourself, an actual sexual lubricant is the way to go—water-based if you're using toys, silicone-based if not.

Many of the other chapters in this book reveal that their titular exhortations were metaphorical in nature, or tongue in cheek, or suggestions rather than directives. But what I mean when I say play with your butthole is pretty literal: I do mean play with your butthole. I mean experiment with the pleasure potential of your anus, and get to know a part of your body in the process.

But more than that, I mean it's important to come to terms with your own penetrability if you want to be a real man and not a bunch of puffed-up machismo with the volume turned up. Real, healthy masculinity isn't one that avoids fear, it's one that reckons with it, one that stares fear in the face and sizes it up.

The other consequence of playing with your own asshole, at least once, at least just to see, is that you bridge a gap, however small, between yourself and the concept of homosexuality. Whatever your sexuality—maybe you are gay and this whole chapter is nothing new to you; maybe you're as straight as khaki pants—there's little more pernicious than ignorance. In playing with your asshole you're experiencing, just for a moment, a little tiny bit of queerness. And that is honestly important for young men to do in a culture of what the writer Adrienne Rich called compulsory heterosexuality. Too many people realize too late in life that they weren't straight this whole time. They regret not exploring more. They regret tamping everything down, trimming their own branches to fit into a mould society has made for them.

It's hard to write about this kind of thing in a serious way. To you, it may sound dumb—juvenile, gross, ridiculous—but this is genuinely serious stuff. If you're a guy, there's a good chance you know very little about that part of your body, and that has consequences in a number of different ways. There's the pleasure potential you're skipping over, and there's the poor wiping techniques and the resultant stains, the short-term health consequences, like hemorrhoids, and there's the long-term health consequences, like colon cancer.

The prospect of someone sticking anything up there—even a doctor—is so scary that many men would much rather court death than experience that kind of penetration. It's not physical pain they're afraid of—it's the psychological pain of reckoning with their failure to live up to a story that told them that men can't be weak, that being penetrated is weak because that's for women, and that to be effeminate is the worst thing a man can do. As if that's so much more embarrassing than dying decades before your time because you were too macho to get tested for colon cancer.[117] As Jordan Peterson reminds his readers in *12 Rules for Life*, "Not even the best-lived life provides an absolute defense against vulnerability."[118] If you must be vulnerable sometimes—and you must—then lean into it.

---

117   Paul Ritvo, Ronald E. Myers, Lawrence Paszat, Mardie Serenity, Daniel F. Perez, and Linda Rabeneck, "Gender differences in attitudes impeding colorectal cancer screening," BMC Public Health, May 24, 2013, https://www.ncbi.nlm.nih.gov/pmc/articles/PMC3672022/.
118   Peterson.

11

~~no man should ever~~
wear makeup

"What, in fact, is required of a real man? The repression of emotions and the silencing of sensitivity. Being ashamed of gentleness or vulnerability. . . . Dressing in dull colors, always wearing the same pair of drab shoes, not having fun with his hair, not wearing too much jewelry, or any make-up. . . . Not taking much care of his body. Subjecting himself to the brutality of other men without complaint. Knowing how to defend himself, even if he is a sweet person. Being cut off from his femininity, just as women abandon their masculinity, not in response to situation or personality but because society demands it."

—Virginie Despentes, *King Kong Theory*

Culture, at times, can feel like a long list of men's exploits. As I explored in Chapter 1, men are so often the stars of our stories, and when those stories are filmed, real-life men need to play the part of the fictional men we revere. But for all the men I've seen on screen, the men I aspired to be, thrilled to watch, or loved to hate, perhaps none embodies the over-the-top ridiculousness of contemporary North American masculinity like Ron Swanson.

Swanson, one of the primary characters in the NBC sitcom *Parks and Recreation*, which ran from 2009 to 2015, is one of contemporary television's most traditionally masculine characters, portrayed as an over-the-top hodgepodge of traits gesturing towards a stodgy American manhood. He loves red meat, hates feelings and wants to be able to fix things in his woodshop in peace.

The actor Nick Offerman's persona (in real life, he's into woodworking and Scotch, and really does sport a powerful moustache) gives the role a deep believability, but his off-screen progressive views on masculinity[119] likely made him more comfortable with portraying gender role reversals on screen.

In "How a Bill Becomes a Law," episode three from season five of the show, there's a genuinely fascinating moment that I want to explore, because it feels like such a beautiful window into healthy masculinity. In this particular episode, in the process of fixing a pothole, Ron and his younger coworker Andy (Chris Pratt) meet the woman who called to have it fixed, Diane (Lucy Lawless) as well as her young daughters. While Ron is initially put off by the girls' princess-themed playfulness, Andy jumps right in and

---

119   Jeremy Hobson, "Nick Offerman On Masculinity, Megan Mullally And Not Being Ron Swanson," WBUR, November 4, 2019, https://www.wbur.org/hereandnow/2019/11/04/nick-offerman-not-ron-swanson.

is quickly covered in makeup, dubbing himself Princess Rainbow Sparkle. Though Ron scoffs at this display, he's eventually roped into it, begrudgingly allowing the girls to make him up in over-the-top pink and turquoise face paint. Though he gets embarrassed when Diane laughs at his new look, his willingness to play along (as well as Andy's excitement to take part) is an incredible example of progressive masculinity. And when Diane turns the tables by asking him out for dinner later in the episode, he's not too proud to accept with a smile. Small wonder that (spoiler alert!) Diane ends up marrying him in the next season.

~

One of the funny things about men's deep-seated fear of makeup is how common its use is in the very places men turn for masculine inspiration: movies and TV and celebrities. The tough guys so valorized in North American culture over the past century or so have all been carefully made-up by teams of people whose job it's been to ensure they look just right—their hair in place, their moustaches expertly trimmed, their shirt sleeves elegantly rolled. They don't saunter in front of the cameras having just rolled out of bed; they sit in a chair in front of a mirror for an hour or two to make sure their just-rolled-out-of-bed look is just right. Their faces, their hair, their overall looks must tell a story, one that the audience will lap up without question. In short, they're no different in that respect than the female stars, whose makeup must tell a similar, if different story—one of beauty, of grace, of desirability.

I brought that *Parks and Recreation* scene up because it feels emblematic of a few things—the way manly men are expected to disdain and avoid things like princesses, rainbows and sparkles, for one, but also the way knowing when it's OK to engage in them can, in fact, benefit you in the long run. Ron might be the most macho TV character you'll ever see—and again, his looks are just as polished as any woman's on the show—but within the narrative, being willing to temper his rugged masculinity with a little playfulness and letting these two young girls' love of makeup (literally) rub off on him helped him find the love of his life.

Of course, the story's fictional—it's a TV sitcom. But the fear of makeup, of pink, of dresses and skirts and anything that remotely might suggest one of these feminine things isn't. It's a very real force in the lives of men and boys, one that's powerful while also being so unspoken that it's almost invisible. It's also a very time- and place-specific phenomenon, which might not be readily apparent. It's far from uniquely North American, but it does feel like one that's bound up in the power of Hollywood and the American fashion industry, and in the historical socio-political dominance of the colonial powers of Europe.

The two- and three-piece suits that have been the dominant male outfit for centuries now are specific outcrops of European culture. They are not the only way men can dress, nor the only way men should dress. Kurtas, worn by South Asian men, for instance, replace the blazer with a conceptually very different top—you have to take it off over your head, rather than just slipping it off your arms.

I wore one once, for a Sikh wedding where I was part of the bridal party, and it opened my eyes in very real ways to the potential of different ways to dress.

If you think about it, even pants aren't all that special. Humans have been wearing them for centuries, but they're not the only way to cover your legs, and in many climates and cultures, covering one's legs isn't necessarily the best option, anyway. As the skort proves, the line between short pants and skirts is a malleable one, and as all the burly Scottish men wearing kilts prove, the gender of the skirt is flexible.

But the variety of ways men can dress we see all over the world should be inspirational—the only real fashion rules are the ones in our heads. You can spend your whole life locked into the familiar straitjacket of North American menswear if that's what you really want, but it's also worth exploring whether that's what you really want, after all.

~

Like many young guys, I spent most of my teens and 20s with no clear understanding of how I wanted to look. However, unlike some guys, who genuinely don't care about their clothes or their overall appearance, for me it wasn't that at all. I wanted badly, on some level, to look nice, to like the way I looked—I simply didn't understand what I needed to do to get there, and never felt brave enough to start figuring it out in a strategic way. Fashion seemed to come to me sideways, in fits and starts and moments of accident. The clothes I wore, the hairstyles

I adopted, the accessories I did make use of—it all felt haphazard and stilted. I don't think I really got a sense of how to look the way I wanted, holistically, until I was about 30.

It's hard for me, now, not to look back and regret that fact, particularly when I revisit old photos I'm in. I wish I could go back in time and explain fashion and grooming to my younger self. Younger Alex was afraid to investigate, to explore, to experiment. I wasted a lot of time looking boring, or stupid, or bad because I didn't know any better, and the idea of finding out felt fraught and scary. My father wasn't a fashion role model; clothing was expensive and I didn't have much money; I was socially anxious and walking into stores scared me; online clothes shopping was still in its infancy and the prospect of having to return an ill-fitting order felt overwhelming; and thrift shops, with their racks and racks of aging, forgotten merchandise, imbued me with such a profound sadness that I could never seriously imagine going to one to look for clothes I'd then wear proudly.

My hair, especially, was a source of unvoiced anxiety. Specific attempts to experiment with my look were met with mockery. In my first year of high school, I tried to gel my hair up, spiking it in the front, but a cooler kid than me insisted on ridiculing it. Near the end of my teens, I asked my hairdresser for a mohawk, but hated how it turned out, and, as it was raining, rubbed the gel out of my hair as I walked home, vowing to leave it unspiked, telling myself I liked it. (An older male coworker at the grocery store, upon seeing the resulting look for the first time, asked me if I'd lost a bet.) I never felt comfortable in hair salons. I'd grown up going to a very female-coded one where my mother was a regular, but felt out of place there; still, going to barbershops, where a vague scent of macho posturing felt like it hung in the air, always set me on edge. So I never really figured out how to approach my hair—which is especially fine and needs some kind of product to stay in place—until my 30s. There are vacation photos of me from my mid-20s where the wind has blown my hair over my eyes. I look ridiculous, which ruins the memory a little bit. I was working at the world's leading men's site at the time. I had access to people who understood hair and how to make it do what you wanted. I just never had the courage to ask anyone for help.

Of course, turning 30 doesn't mean anything in particular, but for me, it was a sort of sea change, a time when I shifted from one long-term relationship into singledom and then into another relationship. A few months after my 30th birthday, I left my full-time role as an AskMen editor to become a freelancer; I now worked from home and, as so many things in my life were changing, I finally had an opportunity to spend some more time consciously considering my appearance. I remembered that, as a teenager, I'd taken pleasure in painting my nails white with a bottle of Liquid Paper, or black with Sharpie markers, and I started experimenting with nail polish. I remembered that, as a child, I'd loved trying on my mother's clip-on earrings and ordered some online. I realized that I'd always wanted to have nice hair and finally got mine professionally dyed. I felt good about myself, how I looked. I was starting to look like the self I felt like inside, not the self that had been imposed on me my whole life, that I'd grabbed on to out of fear. I wasn't leaving every aspect of masculine presentation behind—I was just re-evaluating why I'd been doing what I'd been doing.

So much of masculinity is holding on to things we were taught out of fear. Fear that if we stray too far, we'll be punished. Cast out, sanctioned, insulted, abused, beaten up. Sometimes, those fears are valid. Men do act cruelly towards other men for violating these rules. But we're also in a period when things are shifting. The winds of change are at our backs. Taking a chance on something like wearing nail polish, for instance, is less dangerous than it might have been a few decades ago. And nothing helps shift the culture like individual people, en masse, making new and unexpected decisions. Until the narrow-minded bullies find that they're distinctly in the minority and start wondering if maybe they, too, should try wearing some makeup.

~

Of course, as any woman will tell you, caring about your looks is not some fun, happy free-for-all that's solely about exploring your own unique sense of style and never being criticized. For women, beauty is something they're taught they must maintain or chase essentially from the moment they're born. Beauty culture can lead to anorexia, bulimia, low self-esteem, self-harm, even suicide—but this book isn't about young women, so I won't go into more detail about them. I will say I believe there's a reason that, when teenage girls break the law—which they do at much lower rates than boys[120]—shoplifting looms large, particularly shoplifting of beauty products.[121] Like boys, they're victims of a story. So often, they're taking the beauty products they feel they need to achieve the looks they've been socialized to believe are mandatory. Unending, intense social pressure will make people do almost anything to fit in.

Similarly, the primary negative impact of looks-based cruelty on boys and men is when they don't live up to increasingly stratified and aestheticized male standards—when they don't look enough like muscle-bound bodybuilders or Hollywood movie stars.

The unhealthy relationship between media representations and body image that's so destructive for women has now migrated into male territory. As Jack Myers puts it in his 2016 book, *The Future of Men*, "Congratulations, men, and welcome to the world of societal pressures to conform to body images that are unrealistic and cause you to desperately purchase cosmetics, beauty aids, and diet products because you don't look like that beautiful model in that commercial."[122]

120   Statistics Canada, "Persons accused of police-reported crime for selected offences, by sex of the accused, Canada, 2017," 2019, https://www150.statcan.gc.ca/n1/pub/85-002-x/2019001/ article/00001/tbl/tbl02-eng.htm.

121   EJ Dickson, "Shoplifting and the Teen Girl: What, how, and why middle class teens steal," *Racked*, October 26, 2016, https:// www.racked.com/2016/10/26/13175722/shoplifting-teen-girl -middle-class-psychology.

122   Jack Myers, *The Future of Men: Masculinity in the Twenty-First Century* (San Francisco: Inkshares, 2016).

Unfortunately, Myers is right on the money. In the past decade, North America has seen surging numbers of men getting plastic surgery. We see services offering fake beard implants to help guys who can't grow a thick beard embody the Brooklyn hipster look. We get bigorexia and other forms of muscle-related male body dysmorphia, as I discussed briefly in Chapter 8, and sprawling social media empires devoted to the sacred pursuit of helping men get ripped at any cost. We see incels on online forums like Reddit alleging that sexual attractiveness is a question of jawline, suggesting that altering the shape of your jawbone by a handful of millimetres in one direction or another is the key to sexual success and thus, happiness. Men are finding out the hard way what women have known for a long time—what it's like to feel too keenly the gap between how you look and how you want to look, how you think you should look, how you're told you should look.

But you can't fight something you don't understand. It's past time for men to recognize that, though women bear the brunt of a visuals-obsessed culture that pushes everyone to conform to a single, unreachable beauty standard, they, too, are impacted by its effects in increasingly ugly ways, both physically and psychologically. If Barbie dolls—whose jarringly unrealistic proportions are accepted as an ideal—are giving girls the wrong idea about how thin and feminine they should look, is it any wonder that G.I. Joe action figures, whose muscles have become increasingly unrealistic over the past few decades, as Jackson Katz points out in the 2013 documentary *Tough*

Guise 2, are giving boys the wrong idea about how strong and masculine they should look?[123]

~

Of course, you might say, if women's relationship to beauty is so unhealthy, and men are increasingly seeming to emulate it, why on earth are you pushing for men to start taking up something like makeup, so central to notions of female beauty? Doesn't that feel like adding insult to injury?

But, body dysmorphia aside, most men aren't driving themselves crazy pursuing an unrealistic standard. Wearing makeup may be part of the game for women, but it isn't for men, which means that pushing for men to step outside of the strictly masculine look is asking them to push back against the one-size-fits-all mentality that is slowly poisoning our culture. It's asking them to think with a bit more intentionality about how they really want to look, and why, and until you explore options outside of navy, black and grey, or big and muscular, or bearded and angry, you might just never find out.

Currently, it seems like guys need some inarguable facet of masculinity locked down to dabble in the slightest female-coded aspects of their look. Rich white frat bros can wear a pink polo. Muscle-bound bouncers can wear a stud in their ears. Pro hockey players can grow their hair long. Daredevil skateboarders can dye their hair blond. It's like you need to be able to beat up, ostracize

---

123   Media Education Foundation, *Tough Guise 2*, 2013.

or humiliate anyone who might question your masculinity before exploring outside of its rigid confines. Why?

When people talk about fragile masculinity, stuff like this comes to mind. That so many men are so damn scared of being perceived, even for a moment, even by a person or two, as beautiful, because beauty is feminine and women are weak and bad. Who would men be if they weren't afraid? What would they be capable of if the fear of straying from the herd was not hemming in their every thought, word and deed?

As trans artist Vivek Shraya says in her 2018 memoir, *I'm Afraid of Men,*

> Your fear is not only hurting me, it's hurting you, limiting you from being everything you could be. Consider how often you have dismissed your own appearance, behaviours, emotions, and aspirations for being too feminine or masculine. What might *your life* be if you didn't impose these designations on yourself, let alone on me?
>
> What if you were to challenge yourself every time you feel afraid of me—and all of us who are pushing against gendered expectations and restrictions? What if you cherished us as archetypes of realized potential? What if you were to surrender to sublime possibility—yours and mine? Might you then free me at last of my fear, and of your own?[124]

---

124   Vivek Shraya, *I'm Afraid of Men* (Toronto: Penguin, 2018).

Wouldn't you be something closer to a real man if you could wear a skirt, or a dress, or lipstick, even once, to try it out, and see how it felt, or even as a joke, and not feel terrified that you were somehow breaking a secret man promise? Wouldn't you be closer to a real man if you could invest in skincare and have routines to take care of how your body looks and feels and ages without worrying that some narrow-minded bro—or worse, your buddies—will make fun of them? Wouldn't you be kind of like Ron Swanson letting Diane's daughters make him up in pink and sparkles?

So much of our lives is regimented by rules and laws we didn't agree to and pressures we can only dimly perceive. Why should your brief, precious time on this earth be so drab, and bland, and so undermoisturized? No one should be afraid to dance, and no one should be afraid to look their best, consigned their whole lives long to wearing clothing that looks like the fabric equivalent of the uniformly grey and boxy PC computers in the '90s, or worse.

As the author Michael Chabon writes in his 2009 memoir-in-essays, *Manhood for Amateurs*, "I was once informed by a mother of my acquaintance, half disapprovingly, that wearing a pink shirt was a brave thing for a man to do. It's simply the case that as I get older, I seem every day to give a little bit less of a fuck what people think of or say about me."[125] Chabon is open about the ways in which he doesn't particularly conform to any macho man

---

125   Michael Chabon, *Manhood for Amateurs: The Pleasures and Regrets of a Husband, Father, and Son* (New York: HarperCollins, 2009).

stereotypes in his book, but he's not exactly enamored of feminine signifiers. He simply understands that there is something valuable, something strong, something, dare I say, manly, in not caring what other people think, in crossing a line and exploring.

So when I say wear makeup, what I mean is, it's not too late to break through your deep-seated fear of looking even the slightest bit feminine and experiment. It's not too late to leave behind the notion that to look nice—to look special, to look fancy—is something that men aren't allowed to have, that to want to sparkle is sissified, that to care about your appearance is superficial. And what I also mean is: it's time that we, as a society, muddy the waters about how gender is supposed to look. Maybe it's time that we start giving cover for trans people to experiment, so that someone raised as a boy can wear a dress without anyone freaking out about it. Because maybe it's time for guys all over the world to experience the freeing feeling that Scottish men have known for hundreds of years—the sensation of the wind on their legs as it whips their skirts around—and decide for themselves how they feel about it.

12

~~how much of a man can you be if you~~ let women talk down to you

"Assume that the person you are listening to might know something you don't."

—Jordan B. Peterson, *12 Rules for Life*

Like many talkative, opinionated young boys, my first model for conversation was the way my mother would listen to me. Both of my parents worked, but my mother, a freelance translator, worked from home, which meant she was always around, and though she was often busy, we could speak to each other when needed, without barriers. The foundation of our parent-child relationship was lengthy discussions about anything and everything. As far back as I can remember, I had a very close relationship with her, and, sometimes to a fault, felt like I could tell her anything, because I knew she would listen.

At times, that dynamic felt almost parodic. Though we didn't have a TV when I was growing up, as I got older and started watching movies on my own, I'd come home so entranced by them that I had to tell her everything, and on more than a few occasions, my recounting of the film's plot took so long it could nearly rival the film's runtime itself. In short, I was exposed, from a young age through the beginning of my adulthood, to the ever-attentive ear of a woman who always seemed ready to listen to what I had to say, to consider my opinion, to prioritize the sharing of my anecdotes and feelings above her own.

This is far from a unique scenario, and in many cases, it's a gendered dynamic, not unlike the one I explored in Chapter 2, where young girls are often socialized to take care of chores in ways both big and small, and boys are not. This is the gender divide at work again: we expect boys to grow up to be smart—leaders and philosophers and writers—so we treat them like their opinions matter long before they have anything particularly intelligent to say, while subtly treating girls differently. We praise boys for their bravery and girls for their prettiness, and, because kids are smarter than we give them credit for—as I'll explore a bit more in the next chapter—they intuit societal expectations accordingly.

I don't know that my parents treated my sister any differently than they did me, but each time our young eyes and ears took in sexist, gendered representations of female and male out in the world, and registered them as "like me" or "not like me," we were building up an unspoken understanding of our future roles as speaker and listener, respectively.

I bring this up because I—and many progressive, feminist men I know—struggle to this day with shutting up and listening. It's not anecdotal and it's not biological—it's socialization at work. If you were socialized male, there's a good chance you weren't expected to sit quietly while the women talked, the same way there's a good chance you weren't expected to do your own laundry or wash your own dishes. Being bad at listening doesn't make you a horrible person—it just makes you someone with a glaring weakness who needs to start fixing it.

I feel like my journey towards being a good listener began with making female friendships in high school—my friend Melissa, who I wrote about in Chapter 1, chief among them. Seeing myself as a friendless nerd, and desperate for connection, I came to those friendships with a certain amount of humility, and it allowed me to learn. That's not to say that I let them walk all over me; I was still very convinced of my own brilliance, and I'm certain, in retrospect, that I acted like I knew much more than I did on numerous occasions. But I managed not to alienate them with the privileged tendency to take one's own thoughts much more seriously than those of others. I recognized in those girls an intelligence, an awareness of things that I didn't yet know, and I treated it like it mattered. If I hadn't, I shudder to think of where I might be now. Melissa basically led me by the hand to the creative writing program I'd attend, and a friend she introduced me to, Vanessa, almost literally led me by the hand to the student newspaper's office for the first time. My creative writing degree and my experience working for that paper are the foundation of my career as a writer, and I owe these parts of my life in very real ways to help from women who were more confident and knowledgeable than me.

That mentality of humility around other people's expertise is important, because life is much more often a question of teamwork than going it alone. If you've ever played a trivia-based team game before—like, say, pub trivia, or something in school like Reach for the Top—you understand the importance of diversity, even if you may not think of it as such. There is nothing less useful than a team of four people who all know the exact same things. Your intimate knowledge of your favourite team's championship wins in decades past is dead weight if your buddy sitting next to you also knows it by heart, but neither of you know anything about the structure of nucleic acids when a chemistry question comes up. On the other hand, throw together a music nerd, a history buff, a science geek and a sports fanatic with a penchant for watching classic cinema and you have the makings of a solid roster. None of you will know everything, but each of you knows many things the others do not. You patch up the holes in each other's knowledge bases. Your diversity is your strength.

There's a famous quote, typically described simply as African folk wisdom, though its origins are disputed,[126] that feels apt here: "If you want to go fast, go alone. If you want to go far, go together." It's a pat, pithy saying, but the reason it gets repeated so often is that there is a certain wisdom to it. It's true that other people will

---

126   Andrew Whitby, "Who First Said: If You Want to Go Fast, Go Alone; if You Want to Go Far, Go Together?" December 25, 2020, https://andrewwhitby.com/2020/12/25/if-you-want-to-go-fast/.

slow you down or otherwise hinder your progress in lots of circumstances, but meaningful success is almost never possible without a team. And if your mind jumps to examples of solo successes—star tennis players, or singer/songwriters who left their bands to strike it out alone, for instance—I have some bad news for you about where success comes from. Remember Adam Smith and his meals, from Chapter 2? That star tennis player has a coach, and a trainer, and a sports psychologist at her disposal. That rock star has an agent, a manager, a music producer and a giant record company promotion apparatus to thank. Have you ever seen anyone win an Oscar or a similar award on TV before? They get onstage and start thanking other people.

Nobody's success happens in a vacuum, because it's impossible to do everything yourself, and we all need other people to support, guide, encourage and teach us. And this is a lifelong process. When we're born, human babies are some of the least useful creatures on the planet. Horses and elephants can practically walk right out of the womb; whales and dolphins literally swim out. Humans need incredible amounts of support, nurture and coddling before they're even able to take a baby step, let alone talk, read or write.

As adults, we are equally vulnerable, though the propaganda of masculine ideology would have you believe otherwise if you're a man. The myths of the solitary superhero, the lone cowboy, the reclusive genius have all been branded into our minds by the cultures we live in by the time we're old enough to vote. Heart attacks, strokes, car crashes—our lives can all change drastically in an instant, and the idea that we can weather any and all disasters on our own is short-sighted at best and deeply dangerous at worst.

It's thinking like this that lies at the root of people, too often men, who are unwilling to, for instance, curtail their personal behaviour to benefit society as a whole, as we saw all too clearly during the pandemic, when stereotypically masculine, libertarian, independence-minded cultures like the United States struggled much more than others to contain the virus's spread.

~

One of the worst aspects of this mentality is men's unwillingness to consider what women have to say. Rather than seeing women as a team member with a different skill set, too many guys see them as the enemy, someone to be distrusted, avoided, argued with or defeated. Of course, there's a word now that gets at the kind of thing I'm describing—men refusing to listen to women and insisting on talking over them. It's called mansplaining—a term that emerged in 2008, inspired by Rebecca Solnit's essay "Men Explain Things to Me"—as a means of describing a pre-existing phenomenon that all too many women were familiar with, when men explain things to them that they already know, often better than the man explaining does. But while Solnit's now-iconic tale of having her own book explained to her at a party by a bloviating man who'd read a single review of it tapped into the culture as a powerful anecdote, it is backed up by data.

Studies have shown that men are much more confident than women when it comes to sharing their opinions. Further, we do seem to have a cultural issue with women talking, period. One infamous study found that, in situations where women spoke exactly half of the time, listeners felt the conversation was dominated by the women.[127] As the Australian writer Dale Spender puts it, "The talkativeness of women has been gauged in comparison not with men but with silence. Women have not been judged on the grounds of whether they talk more than men, but of whether they talk more than silent women."[128] We have societal expectations that men will speak and women will listen, and, at its most egregious, it leads to a whole lot of smart women standing around frustrated while men jabber away about things they barely understand.

Then there's the way many men conduct themselves in conversation with women. As with mansplaining, in recent years, people have started to notice the "devil's advocate" position that lots of guys take when debating things they have no real stake in, like, say, women's rights. But even though people push back on this more often these days, we often don't see what a destabilizing choice it is.

---

127 Anne Cutler and Donia R. Scott, "Speaker sex and perceived apportionment of talk," *Applied Psycholinguistics*, 1990, https://pure.mpg.de/rest/items/item_68785_7/component/file_506904/content.
128 Dale Spender, *Man Made Language* (Milton Park: Routledge & Kegan Paul, 1980).

As the French writer Pauline Harmange puts it in her 2020 book, *I Hate Men*, "Men who choose the terrain of reason, as opposed to emotion, place themselves in a position of authority. Only someone in a position of dominance can permit himself to be calm and reasonable in any circumstance, because he's not the one who is suffering. It's a choice not to hear the emotions of an interlocutor—the choice of not wanting to understand the other side of the story, and of refusing to envisage the possibility that one might bear any responsibility for it."[129]

If you listen to some men, the real problem may simply be women's voices, period. In Anne Carson's essay "The Gender of Sound," published in her seminal 1995 book, *Glass, Irony & God*, she explores the ways men have complained about having to listen to the sounds women make throughout history, the uncanny way critiques of the female voice have synched up across cultures and centuries.

"Their sounds are bad to hear and make men uncomfortable," Carson writes. "Just how uncomfortable may be measured by the lengths to which Aristotle is willing to go in accounting for the gender of sound physiognomically; he ends up ascribing the lower pitch of the male voice to the tension placed on a man's vocal chords by his testicles functioning as loom weights."

Later in the essay, she explores the ways in which men dream of shutting women's high-pitched vocals up: "Putting a door on the female mouth has been an important project of patriarchal culture from antiquity to the present

---

129   Pauline Harmange, *I Hate Men* (New York: HarperCollins, 2020).

day. Its chief tactic is an ideological association of female sound with monstrosity, disorder and death."[130]

It's no real shock, then, to recognize that the major contemporary complaints about speech patterns are often gendered ones. Things like vocal fry and uptalk, as the linguist Amanda Montell explores in her 2019 book, *Wordslut: A Feminist Guide to Taking Back the English Language*, have been treated as though they're the worst crimes you can commit when opening your mouth, though they are, ultimately, incredibly benign modulations of speech that pale in comparison to the differences, say, between a Texas accent and a British one.

But which came first, men's fear of women's voices or their fear of the kinds of things women say, or might say? If sound was the only issue, wouldn't men embrace women discussing things soundlessly online or in print? As you may know, men aren't inclined to read women at higher rates than they listen to them.

And it isn't just women labelled harpies, banshees, witches, bitches, crones and hags that get this treatment. Oddly, many men seem uninterested in hearing the voices of even the women they're attracted to. In the hookup-crazed era that was the second half of the 2010s, people were going on a lot of bad dates, dates where men displayed zero interest in hearing what women had to say. As the writer Madeleine Holden explores in an aptly titled 2018 piece for *MEL* magazine called "The Depressing Phenomenon of Men Who Ask Their Dates No Questions," such a divide

---

130   Anne Carson, "The Gender of Sound," *Glass, Irony & God* (New York: New Directions Books, 1995).

could be a question of nerves, or social awkwardness. But the fact that, anecdotally, it is almost always women on the receiving end—and even more often men on the giving end—of these non-questions suggests a gendered issue.

Holden goes on to note some of the women who've experienced this mused that "men in general [might be] more likely to view dates as a personal marketing exercise ('Here's why you should find me attractive') rather than an opportunity to get to know a romantic prospect," and that feels accurate to me, based on what I know about men in a romantic and/or sexual context. They aren't interacting with a person, they're acting out a script. [131]

If they recognize what's happening at all, these men may see this as simply good business, or they may see "brag about yourself" as a life raft to cling to in the sea of uncertain first-date conversation. Women subjected to this kind of treatment tend to see it as at least a bit dehumanizing. It's possible to ask someone questions without caring about them or their response, but even a handful of questions (What do you do for a living? What have you been up to lately? How do you like a certain cuisine or genre of music?) certainly goes a lot further down the "I see you as a human being" path than simply talking at someone about yourself.

~

131   Madeleine Holden, "The Depressing Phenomenon of Men Who Ask Their Dates No Questions," *MEL*, https://melmagazine. com/en-us/story/the-depressing-phenomenon-of-men-who-ask-their-dates-no-questions.

The quintessentially male insistence on his own knowledge, his own expertise and, by contrast, the ignorance and inadequacy of women, has far-reaching consequences. Michael Chabon, in *Manhood for Amateurs*, muses at length on this issue's ramifications at the level of both the personal and the political:

> I have no doubt that the male impulse to downplay his own lack of fitness for a job, to refuse to acknowledge his inadequacy, insufficiency, or lack of preparation, has been and continues to be responsible for a large share of the world's woes, in the form of the accidents, errors, and calamities that result from specific or overarching acts of faking it, a grim encyclopedia of which the G. W. Bush administration readily affords. There is also the more subtle damage that is done repeatedly to boys who grow up learning from their fathers and the men around them the tragic lesson that failure is not a human constant but a kind of aberration of gender, a flaw in a man, to be concealed.
>
> Men's refusal to stop and ask for directions, a foundational cliché of women's criticism, analysis, and stand-up mockery of male behavior, is a perfect example of this tendency to put up a front, in that it views as aberrant a condition—being lost—that is ineluctable, a given of human existence. We are born lost and spend vast stretches of our lives on wrong turns and backtracking. In this respect, male fronting resembles a number of other behaviors

typically ascribed to men and masculinity, in that it proceeds by denying essential human conditions or responses—say public displays of mutual affection, grief, or triumph—marking them as feminine, infantile, socially unacceptable.[132]

I think the point he makes at the end is an important one. This game that men engage in is one of willful ignorance, a refusal to acknowledge that they are human, fallible and imperfect, and that has a certain soul-crushing quality to it. But let's take a second to consider the other point—the point that there are real and tangible consequences to the default assumption that men always know what they're doing, even when they don't.

As Ijeoma Oluo puts it in her 2020 book, *Mediocre*, rewarding privileged people for mediocrity is a dangerous game for both the haves and the have-nots: "The rewarding of white male mediocrity not only limits the drive and imagination of white men; it also requires forced limitations on the success of women and people of color in order to deliver on the promised white male supremacy."[133]

Oluo's mention of whiteness is important, because gender is not the only arena where people in a dominant group ignore the wisdom of those less privileged, to their detriment, and sometimes peril. In his 2021 book, *Fear of a Black Universe: An Outsider's Guide to the Future of Physics*, Stephon Alexander explores this dynamic through

---

132 Chabon.
133 Ijeoma Oluo, *Mediocre: The Dangerous Legacy of White Male Power* (London: Basic Books, 2021).

a racial lens, expanding it to include the dominant culture's distrust of any kind of outsider-dom, and then waxing lyrical on the benefits of having an outsider's perspective:

> Outsiders who craft nonconventional ideas and develop new techniques, similar to graffiti, can be seen as vandals, and that "vandalism" may be penalized. Innovating outside the mainstream is hugely risky. However, the realization that some forms of deviance result in positive accomplishments was a game changer for me. . . . [M]any significant innovations in science came from someone who was an outsider in a given field, someone who applied a new technique or perspective from another field. Perhaps this was because they were valued within both disciplines. Perhaps it is time to value and elevate minorities, thus enabling them to make major contributions, not in spite of their outsider's perspective, but because of it.[134]

Conservatives, who seem to enjoy claiming victimhood when they're in fact quite powerful, like to talk about "diversity of opinion" in recent years. It's a way of saying "we think that right-wing white people should be included in groups of liberal white people, and that's as important or more important than including people of colour" without saying all of that explicitly. But what they miss when they parrot talking points about "diversity of opinion" is that coming

---

134   Stephon Alexander, *Fear of a Black Universe: An Outsider's Guide to the Future of Physics* (New York: Basic Books, 2021).

from a vastly different background—say, from another country, another culture, another race, another gender—is an incredibly important way to develop a different point of view.

Genuine diversity—like the natural biodiversity we find in forests, not the manicured diversity of a giant farm that grows 20 different kinds of crops in 20 separate pesticide-covered fields—comes from letting people with vastly different life experiences congregate and encouraging them to learn from each other's differences. It's easy to go your whole life completely ignorant of how other people live, think and act, particularly when you're someone who benefits from a privilege that other people do not.

That's how you get able-bodied people who know nothing about disability making architectural decisions that will impact people who use mobility aids, because it doesn't occur to them that not everyone can simply walk with ease. That's how you get rich businesspeople making decisions that will impact poor people without ever considering anything about their lives. And that's how you get cis male politicians banning abortion—a medical procedure none of them have personal experience with—because they feel like their thoughts take precedence over the real consequences for people who actually do get pregnant. For the people behind these decisions, their choices aren't necessarily especially meaningful. But if your life is impacted by the decisions of people who shut out the ideas, opinions and expertise of anyone who doesn't look like them, their choices can be matters of life and death.

Increasingly, I've been feeling like men are a group of people who've spent their whole lives inhaling propaganda for a certain way of life that no longer exists, a black-and-white mentality centred on dominance and violence to the exclusion of care, connection and gentleness—all the things that make life worth living in a harsh universe. Because of that upbringing, they're not yet adapted to seeing the fullness, richness and nuance of certain aspects of life. And that's fine, if you live in a world where those aspects you've been ignoring are and will remain meaningless. But is that this world?

As I'll explore more in the next chapter, the future of masculinity is going to involve a lot of interactions with women where men are, at best, on equal footing, and often they'll find themselves subordinate. Female bosses are no longer a joke punchline, female politicians are getting elected, female entrepreneurs are getting rich quick. Success is no longer the male-dominated space it once was, and men ignoring, talking over, contradicting or otherwise being rude to women is going to be a lot less socially acceptable than it was in decades past. We're past it being normal and we're past it being something people brush off.

If they're smart, men will recognize this before those behaviours harden into habits, because habits are hard to break, and, as we see in the Solnit-esque viral tweets where women recount instances of men trying to mansplain their own work to them, contemporary culture loves taking down a blowhard.

So when I say let a woman talk down to you, what I mean is stop trying to put a door on the mouths of people more feminine than you are. What I mean is recognize that listening is a source of strength, not weakness, that learning from your mistakes and shortcomings is growth, not failure, that being lost and uncertain is a fundamental and necessary part of the human condition, not a failure to be a real man.

. What I mean is that people who are different from you have more to offer than you may realize, and that the masculine ideology that women are annoying, prattling, gossiping, nagging bitches is not only deeply misogynistic, it's also at the root of a lot of things going wrong when they didn't need to, because groups who value the contributions, intelligence and knowledge bases of a diversity of people have a lot fewer weak spots than those who all value the same thing in unison.

That's not just hippie-dippie stuff, either. Even economists—a largely male-dominated field—know that women have untapped value, that more egalitarian companies and nations perform better because they aren't needlessly stifling the output of half of the population. Too often, cishet male–dominated cultures ignore the potential value of contributions from female or queer people, then are bewildered when something—that would have been obvious to someone of a different gender—goes awry. But what's so confusing about that? They're making the same mistake as staffing a trivia team with all science geeks and no sports nerds without even realizing it.

13

act like a woman

"There are plenty of opportunities for men.
Theoretically, they can be anything these days: secre-
tary, seamstress, PTA president."

— Hanna Rosin, *The End of Men*

S ince the American journalist Hanna Rosin adapted
"The End of Men," her 2010 article for *The Atlantic*,
into a full-length book in 2012, the crisis of masculinity
has never felt far from the front pages of a collective
cultural discourse.

It's fascinating to think about the way the present
moment presses down on men's well-being. Part of the
problem, of course, is that many men are grappling with
being members of a newly vilified segment of society.
It's cool, now, to make jokes at men's expense, cool to
say you hate men. Many men are feeling stranded these
days, trying to figure out how to move through the world,
how to feel at home in a culture that's grown more than a
little bit skeptical of them. As a group, they seem not to

have a clear purpose in life, as societal expectations shift beneath their feet.

The dilemma here reminds me, interestingly enough, of what women were facing several decades ago, near the middle of the 20th century, captured by the writer Betty Friedan in her seminal book *The Feminine Mystique*:

> The feminine mystique permits, even encourages, women to ignore the question of their identity. The mystique says they can answer the question "Who am I?" by saying "Tom's wife . . . Mary's mother." But I don't think the mystique would have such power over American women if they did not fear to face this terrifying blank which makes them unable to see themselves after twenty-one. The truth is . . . an American woman no longer has a private image to tell her who she is, or can be, or wants to be.

Now, try rereading the last paragraph and gender-swapping each mention of "feminine" and "women" and female-gendered words with "masculine" and "men" and male-gendered ones. It feels like a viable description of 21st-century North American masculinity: a gender whose self-image is in flux in a way that can feel downright terrifying.

As Friedan goes on to say, the image many women had of themselves at the time was a mediated one, constructed "in the magazines and television commercials" to sell products to them. It gained its multi-million dollar economic power, according to Friedan, from a simple fact: "American women no longer know who they are."[135] They could no longer look to their mothers to provide guidance, because they were living in a very different world than the old one their mothers had lived in.

It strikes me that young men today have a lot in common with women in the middle of the 20th century, when Friedan wrote those lines. They're facing a moment of transition and confusion, one that has robbed them of a clear path forward. They are in the midst of an upheaval that is changing everything they know. They are the inheritors of their own "problem that has no name," as Friedan called the thing afflicting (primarily white) mid-century American housewives.

They cannot look to their fathers for guidance, or older men generally; most of them have few if any male role models in their lives. They are interns, not apprentices; mutuals, not friends. The shape and thrust of contemporary life has robbed them of so many avenues of genuine connection, and the ideals of toxic masculinity have cauterized off the rest. They are alone, confused and actively being lied to about who they are, what they should do and what is important in life. No wonder things aren't going so well; no wonder they don't feel great about themselves. But what, exactly, is to be done to fix this sad state of affairs?

~

---

135   Friedan.

In their 2021 book, *The Dawn of Everything*, the anthropologist David Graeber (whose work I've previously mentioned in Chapters 3 and 8) and his co-author, David Wengrow, explore the idea of "schismogenesis" and the prominent role they believed it might play in human culture throughout history. Though it may sound complex, schismogenesis is an anthropological term, coined in the mid-1930s by Gregory Bateson, essentially to describe the practice of creating culture in opposition to other cultures.

Though Bateson was using it in the context of the Iatmul people in New Guinea, Wengrow and Graeber suggest it's possible to see this dynamic at play in all kinds of different levels of human interaction.[136] Think of teens who identify as nerds, in opposition to jocks. Straight-edge punks rebelling against a perceived culture of drugs and booze. Bosses identifying their company's "rival" to foster togetherness among employees. Austin, Texas, whose identity comes from how different it is from the state that surrounds it. Canadians, who identify themselves as "more polite than" Americans. The list goes on. So much of who people are is in opposition to others. We see other people doing things we disagree with or disapprove of, and we construct our own personalities around the opposite.

Sometimes, as in the above examples, this can feel relatively harmless; other times, obviously, it's a strand woven into an ideology of hatred. When there's a power imbalance between two groups, it's not hard to see how defining one

---

136   David Graeber and David Wengrow, *The Dawn of Everything: A New History of Humanity* (New York: Farrar, Straus and Giroux, 2021).

in exact opposition to the other can lead to nasty outcomes. I bring up schismogenesis here because I feel like much of contemporary masculinity, insofar as contemporary masculinity can be considered a coherent ideology or culture, is an act of schismogenesis, one where guys look at what women are doing and start doing the opposite. Women take selfies? Men don't do that. Women wear pink? Men don't do that. Women suck dick? Men definitely don't do that. (This is what underlies the creation of things like "men's yogurt"—corporations trying to fight against the current of schismogenesis in their pursuit of profit.) It's the Man Box from the introduction all over again.

The chapter titles of the book you're reading right now are framed according to this exact logic for a reason. The masculinity we're familiar with is not an ideology of creativity or newness, it's an ideology of rejection and retreat. And that insistence on rejecting what is feminine is biting men in the ass right now because, in the past 50 years or so, femininity has started to associate itself so strongly with hard work and success that men are starting to back away from it. That's why you get commentators like Guy Garcia, who I last cited in Chapter 6, describing men as "a gender that has disidentified with excellence" in *The Decline of Men*, when trying to make sense of the trends of boys struggling in school and men struggling in the workforce.

Exploring this idea, Garcia quotes a Harvard University psychologist named Mahzarin Banaji, and I think it's worth quoting Banaji's thoughts at length here—with one sentence emphasized by me:

[Masculinity] is itself a challenged concept. It's being challenged in every way, from who goes off to war, to who brings home more money, to whom you take directions from at work. Sure, the number of women in male-dominated professions is still small, but their numbers are growing in every sphere of achievement, in nearly every profession. The enclaves that were all male are no longer all male. I can imagine that men today are experiencing something that no other men in the past have. And it's a change that is soft enough, slow enough, that it can't be verbalized. It's not easy to name what's different, that the world isn't as easy as it used to be, as convenient as it was expected to be. *One of the real, and sad, possibilities is that men may disidentify with hard work.* I'm not one to be worrying easily about the shifts in the resources of a privileged group—and I certainly don't mean to imply that I think women control the world's resources!—but I do sense that something is shifting for men. In our thinking about women's rights and women's access to resources, it is important not to lose sight of the fact that men are adjusting to a new world with new power structures and that we ought to be having the conversations to flesh it out, to do research, to prepare for it. The loss of power is never a pretty sight.[137]

137   Garcia.

My last name aside, depending on who you ask, it's arguable that I've been acting like a woman all my life. In part it was just because my parents weren't big on gender policing. Over the years I figured out what was OK and what wasn't for school and in public, like every kid does, but at home I was free to be myself. I wasn't shamed or made to be afraid of any particular mode of expression by my parents. If I cried at my seventh birthday party because, when juice was being poured, another kid got my favourite cup, which was purple, well, that wasn't something to beat out of me. That's just who I was.

Looking back, I owe a lot of who I am now to my parents' willingness to let me be my own person rather than aggressively trying to instill masculine values in me. I played sports, built things out of Lego and didn't take much to pink or Barbies, but those things always felt like my choices rather than things that were prescribed to me. To whatever degree I was indoctrinated by the toxic aspects of masculinity, it was a softer brainwashing than many young boys receive, and easier to undo as I got older.

That doesn't mean I'm entirely free of the shackles of that ideology. I still, for instance, struggle to recognize, name and share my emotions, even if I know that I should. But when I'm in a conversation with my partner and I find myself having trouble expressing my emotions, I don't say, "I'm a man, I can't express my emotions," I say, "I wasn't socialized to express my emotions." This is a minor detail, but an important mental shift. We're no longer talking about an innate difference, an inborn weakness, but a question of practice. Because the truth is that you can get better at things like this with practice.

As the writer Cordelia Fine argues convincingly in her 2010 book, *Delusions of Gender: How Our Minds, Society, and Neurosexism Create Difference*, gender is a social construct far more than it is a question of innate genetic programming. Fine suggests that children are born with a certain sponge-like quality, an innate ability to absorb their surroundings. At the beginning of their lives, that's all they're doing—taking in information. And because gender is such a defining feature of a person for so much of the world, Fine explores the idea that babies and young children are, according to the developmental psychologists Diane Ruble and Carol Martin, "gender detectives"—constantly trying to figure out how gender works and how to correctly place themselves within it according to the rules everyone around them seems to live by.[138]

We know this, on some level—that gender is not biology. That's why some men accuse others of not being "real men"; it's why dads swipe pink toys out of little boys' hands. If men were inherently masculine, a boy could no more become girlish by virtue of playing with dolls than a blue ball could become pink over time by being plunked in an all-pink ball pit. Those sexist dads know that gender is malleable—they know that too much exposure to femininity just might change their sons.

---

138   Cordelia Fine, *Delusions of Gender: How Our Minds, Society, and Neurosexism Create Difference* (New York: W.W. Norton, 2010).

What they don't realize is that this is a good thing, not a bad thing—that, for lack of a better phrase, being in touch with one's feminine side isn't a weakness, but an opportunity, an ability to tap into something many men shy away from. What they don't know is that if their sons could act like women—even a little bit, a little bit of the time—some of the pressure they're holding in, the steam of their emotions, wouldn't be in danger of worsening until it explodes.

~

In his 2017 book, *Kids These Days: Human Capital and the Making of Millennials*, fellow millennial writer Malcolm Harris explores the ways that work has changed in recent years. Though he is writing primarily about the American workforce and labour market, his findings feel broadly applicable to the rest of the Western world. What he saw was an economy where the middle was disappearing—the good jobs are getting better, but the bad jobs (and there are many, many more of those) are getting worse. And this shift is impacting men in a big way, Harris notes: "The missing center of the job distribution, the routine tasks that have been largely mechanized and computerized, were built by and for male workers."

Women, as Harris argues, "are better trained by society for the jobs that have been resistant to automation." Part of the societal training he's talking about is that women are more comfortable, for instance, with performing tasks that involve care and communication and affective labour —essentially, making other people feel nice—but part of the societal training is also, well, the thing that society explicitly does to train people for the workforce: education.[139]

The fact is, writers like Harris, Rosin and Garcia recognize that women have been quietly outperforming men academically for decades, and this is extending to enrolment in higher education in a big way. That college degree advantage is setting them up to have a much bigger share of the job market when they graduate going forward; you don't need to visit the abandoned factories in the Rust Belt to get a sense that the well-paying, unionized labour jobs for men with high school degrees that defined so much of the 20th century in North America just don't exist anymore.

Studies on child development suggest that the gender gap in school is an issue as far back as kindergarten, where boys were found by one study to lag as much as a year behind girls the same age as them in what psychologists and educators term "self-regulation"[140]—which essentially amounts to managing your own impulses in order to pay attention and remembering and implementing behavioural rules. Some commentators believe the way school is structured sets boys up to fail by insisting that they sit still to learn, rather than engaging them kinetically during a time in their lives when they're full of energy. Whether

139   Malcolm Harris, *Kids These Days: Human Capital and the Making of Millennials* (New York: Little, Brown and Company), 2017.
140   Enrico Gnaulati, "Why Girls Tend to Get Better Grades Than Boys Do," *The Atlantic*, September 8, 2014, https://www.theatlantic.com/education/archive/2014/09/why-girls-get-better-grades-than-boys-do/380318/.

this is due to biological factors isn't yet known, but it does seem clear that young boys struggle with passive, quiet learning—and that these struggles do little to help their academic self-confidence going forward. By the time high school rolls around, there are marked differences in the ways boys and girls approach school, from studying to attendance to grades to graduation rates, and even strongholds of supposedly "masculine" skills like math and science show girls overtaking boys in recent decades.

Then they graduate—if they graduate—into a job market ruled by the so-called gig economy, where all workers are replaceable parts in a giant, scaled-up machine, where there are vanishingly few jobs in which can you accomplish things you feel genuinely proud of—especially not in the sense that your male ancestors may have seen things. On top of that, as capitalism is in the process of making all the traditionally masculine jobs disappear via outsourcing, digitizing, streamlining and more, that's not the only way that masculine values are disappearing from the workplace. Consider the story of the oil company in the 1990s that, to reduce workplace accidents on two oil drilling rigs, gave emotional sensitivity training to their almost entirely all-male crews, to help them open up and ask for help—for instance, when they didn't know how to operate the cutting-edge new machinery they were tasked with handling.[141]

---

141   It's a story so perfect that it appears in some form or other in three different books I read while researching this one: Hanna Rosin's *The End of Men*, Lewis Howes's *The Mask of Masculinity* and Liz Plank's *For the Love of Men*.

Or consider a more recent example, like in 2022, when the *New York Times* wrote about a mining company in South Dakota where the mostly male employees wore their love languages on their hard hats to easily communicate the best ways to make them happy.[142] Classical masculinity may be a great fit for certain forms of work—shearing off a person's emotional capacity may seem useful to a boss or a military leader trying to get his men to do dangerous or terrifying or immoral things—but it does not produce healthy human beings capable of handling interactions with other people in day-to-day life. Classic masculinity just doesn't have much of a place in the job market of the future.

That's because capitalism, however much it's associated with masculinity, however much it's embraced by the macho men who love to post inspirational quotes on Instagram and grind and hustle and wear expensive suits, and rejected by the effeminate soy boys, is no ally of masculinity. Capitalism is a force that is interested only in profit, and insofar as that often overlaps with domination, masculinity, as an ideology of power and control, works well with it. But capitalism's interest in profit far outstrips the narrow confines of masculinity. Capitalism doesn't care if you want to be a blacksmith or a cowboy or a woodworker—these days it wants you to be an Uber driver who's afraid to speak lest he lose his five-star rating or an Instacart gig worker scrambling to get an order through in time.

---

142   Emma Goldberg, "Why Your Boss Wants to Know Your Love Language," *New York Times*, March 4, 2022, https://www.nytimes.com/2022/03/04/business/employee-satisfaction-remote-work.html.

From this perspective, capitalism can be a deeply feminizing force, something that strips men's so-called dignity away. As Betty Friedan puts it in *The Feminine Mystique*, "There have been plenty of nonsexual pressures in the America of the last decade—the compromising, never-ceasing competition, the anonymous and often purposeless work in the big organization—that also kept a man from feeling like a man. Safer to take it out on his wife and his mother than to recognize a failure in himself or in the sacred American way of life."[143]

Consider that the vast majority of men no longer own their lives. They spend their hours working at a job they hate just to stay alive; they spend their money on rent because a landlord is the real owner of their home. This is manhood under contemporary capitalism. It's no wonder so many of them turn to libertarian politics—faced with dropping either their lone-wolf masculine ideology or their engagement with society and all its complexities, they choose the latter.

But men will need to reckon with their relationship to capitalism, to jobs and to masculinity sooner rather than later. As Guy Garcia explains in *The Decline of Men*, the concept of the job, the career and the salary are hyper-important to masculine identity:

> One of the pillars of male identity is the ability and willingness to work—to earn money and social status, to help support a wife and family.

---

143   Friedan.

Sociologists and identity theorists agree that for men, work and career are enmeshed with their sense of personal identity and self-esteem. For most men, their performance at work—as bosses or employees—is inextricably connected to their identities as spouses, fathers, and citizens. If men are failing at their jobs, it's harder for them to perceive themselves as good husbands and fathers. In fact, psychologists know that a disruption in any one of these key areas will affect the others. When a man fails to fulfill his roles as an employee, spouse, or father, or if those roles conflict, his entire sense of well-being and worth is undermined.[144]

Retaining that mentality in a world like this one—where good jobs are scarce and what's available are scarcely worth calling jobs, where well-paying careers increasingly go only to the elite and salaries remain stagnant while the cost of living increases—is a dangerous game of chicken. Particularly when men are proving as resistant as they are to taking on jobs that are feminine-coded, while, historically, women have shown no such qualms about taking on male-coded work, in some cases essentially flipping the gender of entire professions, as was the case with secretarial work and school teaching.

~

---

144   Garcia.

In her 2020 book, *Entitled*, Kate Manne explores the male fear of feminine-leaning jobs. As she writes, "Economists have observed that men often prefer unemployment to taking on jobs in nursing (for example, as a nurse's assistant), elder care, or working as a home healthcare aide. Yet these are increasingly the jobs that are available and need doing, as traditionally male blue-collar work disappears from the U.S. economy."

Though Manne acknowledges that female partners often play a role in men's unwillingness to take more feminine jobs, pushing men to hold out for something more stereotypically masculine than nursing, for instance, what's especially gripping is the conclusion she comes to:

> In many communities, especially rural ones, white men are increasingly not working. They are also at increasing risk for depression, drug dependency (especially on opiates), and even suicide. This can plausibly be read as, among other things, the result of a crisis in *meaning*: a lack of fulfilling roles that men have access to in these milieus. Yet care work not only needs doing; it is meaningful, not inherently exploitative, and has other advantages over many forms of traditionally masculine blue-collar labor, in generally tending to be less physically and environmentally damaging. In this case, men's sense of entitlement is not only hurting other vulnerable parties; it is hurting men *themselves*, and standing in the way of solutions

to a gap between role supply and demand that desperately needs filling.[145]

Ultimately, what I mean when I say "act like a woman" is to let go of some of the rigid models of masculinity you've been taught and start valuing flexibility—in your social life, in your professional life, in your life, period. An insistence on "being a man" in the old mode will not get you what you want. Today's men will not be able to time-travel back to the '50s by sheer force of will to enjoy the untrammelled authority of the all-American family man, with his financial power, social cachet and the ability to abuse his wife and control his children. People with penises and testicles and XY chromosomes will be around as long as human beings are. But men who look and act and think like 20th-century men did are a dying breed, because the conditions that allowed for that specific dominance, arrogance and ignorance are disappearing.

You can hold out for the job your forefathers dreamed about all you want, but there's a good chance it won't exist in a decade, if it does at all now. Many of the rugged, "manly" jobs are gone, machined out of existence, and capitalists hell-bent on extracting ever more profits are coming for the ones still hanging on. They don't want to pay you big bucks to look tough and get sweaty. They don't want to pay you at all. Increasingly, most jobs available will be ones that make use of softer skills, and some men will have to get comfortable either working as nurses and

---

145   Kate Manne, *Entitled: How Male Privilege Hurts Women* (New York: Crown, 2020).

caretakers or staying home and doing the unpaid caretaker work while their wives earn the paycheque. Without a broad social program like a universal basic income to ensure no one falls into destitution regardless of whether they have a job or not, the alternatives will be bleak: it's hard not to picture houselessness, substance use and crime, violence and suicide.

It seems to me that in the 21st century, men will be called upon to do what women did in the 19th and 20th centuries—adapt. They're going to have to grapple with a radical reshaping of who and what they can be, and, like the women before them, some of them may find themselves missing certain aspects of the roles they'd grown used to. All the while, they'll experience jeers and criticisms from those who want things to stay the way they were.

And while it's easy to say that that's a dishonest comparison—that the shift women underwent saw them gain concrete things, like the vote, the ability to own property, a greater share of the job market and increasing wages—it's not like men don't have concrete things to gain from a more flexible approach to masculinity. In particular, as I discussed in Chapters 6 and 7, men stand to make enormous gains in terms of their physical and mental health.

It's not hard to imagine a near future where men are coming to terms with a more egalitarian world and are benefitting plentifully from it, where fathers are so invested in their children's lives that it's no longer remarkable, where you're as likely to encounter a male nurse as you are a female doctor, where romantic relationships between partners of all genders feel like everyone is sharing the load equally, where there is enough food and resources for everyone, where physical strength is no longer the important quality it once was and gives way to social arrangements predicated on equality, consent, respect and choice.

what could men do?

"What makes a man? A man makes himself."

—Thomas Page McBee, *Man Alive*

From the age of 25 to 30, I worked on the eighth floor of an office building, and five days a week, week in and week out, month after month, year after year, I took the elevator every morning.

Why wouldn't you? At 19 stairs per floor, eight floors comes out to 152 steps, a prohibitively steep total, no matter how in shape you are. As a society, we invented elevators and planted them at the hearts of our many tall buildings for precisely this reason: to save people the trouble. Because not everyone can climb 152 steps—or even a single one.

But some of us can climb 152 steps, we just don't feel like it. Some of us are young, in the prime of our physical fitness, but choose to take the elevator because it's simpler. Because we're non-athletes, used to using our bodies to move from room to room and not much else. I'd wager that "some of us" is closer to "a lot of us".

About four and a half years into my time at that job, I made a decision. I was going to start climbing. No matter how hard it was, no matter how out of breath I felt when I

241

got to the office, no matter how sweaty it made me, I would climb. I'm not sure why, exactly. Maybe it was the little outcrop of belly that I'd started accumulating. Maybe it felt simpler and cheaper than getting a gym membership.

But I'd climb.

It took a few mornings to stick at first, but within a week or so my instinct to head for the elevators was gone. I would open the door to the stairwell, with 152 steps separating me from my office, take a breath and begin to climb. It was a decision that I'd made, and I was going to stick with it.

~

Let's envision a hypothetical: Two men are drinking. One is drinking beer, the other champagne. Which one's more of a man?

The guy drinking champagne is celebrating a successful business deal. The guy drinking beer can't afford champagne because he was just laid off from a low-paying job. Now which one's more of a man?

But the guy drinking champagne's business deal was to open a beauty salon, while the guy drinking beer was laid off from a factory. Which one's more of a man?

But the guy drinking champagne opened a beauty salon in a partnership with his wife, while the guy drinking beer first got a job at the factory because a man he had a crush on worked there. Which one's more of a man?

But the guy drinking champagne lets his wife peg him in the ass every week, while the guy drinking beer is a top and only fucks other guys in the ass. Which one's more of a man?

By this point in the book, you know the real answer. Neither one is more of a man. Nothing—not the booze you drink, not your career situation, not your chosen field of work, not your relationships, not your sex life—determines how much of a man you are. It's a made-up concept.

You could play this game with any set of characteristics, slowly trying to make people flip-flop on which guy was more of a man with increasingly ridiculous details. There's no up, there's no down, there's no right, there's no wrong. There's just people's opinions, and though they may seem chiselled in stone, they shift from person to person, from generation to generation, from culture to culture. And like a Magic Eye image or an optical illusion, they can shift even within one person's perception. People will jump to find excuses for why something is manly or isn't when what they really mean is: I like this guy and I don't like that guy. And if someone never stops to think deeply about what they like, what they think, who they are or what being a man is really about, well, it doesn't necessarily go any further than that.

That's the power of the myth of masculinity—like Betty Friedan's feminine mystique, it acts as a placeholder for selfhood. It's a ready-made, prefabricated identity. You don't have to work out who you really are deep down—you can be a husband, an employee, a father, a boss; a hard-ass, a chick magnet, a rich guy, a jock.

But what if we, collectively, started trying to imagine masculinity as something with the potential to be more complex? What if we flipped the Man Box inside out and started thinking about all the things men could be, rather than the narrow view of what they can't be? What if we started to expand the definition of masculinity, to recognize that it comes in many shapes and sizes, that it's not tied to your body or your hormones or how you look or dress, that you can possess it without being assigned male at birth and you can be assigned male at birth and not possess an ounce of it, and both are OK?

~

I ask these kinds of questions not just out of academic interest. This kind of stuff is personal to me.

Let me let you in on a secret I've been keeping from you over the course of this book.

I am not a man.

Yes, I was born with a penis and testicles. I still have them. I wear pants, not skirts or dresses, and button-ups, not blouses. When I don't shave my face for a few days I grow stubble, and if I keep it up for a week or more, it turns into a beard, albeit a somewhat patchy one.

If you're someone for whom the gender conversation ends there, well, you probably would say that I *am* a man.

But I'm not. I'm an observer of men, a critiquer of men; someone who devotes a lot of time to thinking about masculinity. Yes, I've been writing for AskMen since 2013, and my last name is Manley. But I do not consider myself a man, and, respectfully, I'd ask you not to consider me one either. What I am is non-binary.

I'd be naive if I said many people wouldn't say that that's made-up, that I'm a man, pure and simple. And as much as I disagree with those people, and as much as I too often start to feel the bite of hate at the edge of their insistence, gender is a social construct. Meaning, it's something that is built, together, by all of us. So when people see me and register me as male because I'm six feet and change tall, they see the ghostly presence of some facial hair and I'm wearing jeans and a T-shirt and a baseball cap, they call me sir, monsieur, bud, guy. I get that. I do perform masculinity a fair amount. When there are only two options, I choose man—whether filling out an online survey or choosing where to piss. So I'm at the very least man-adjacent.

But when there are more than two options, that's when I feel a bit more free to be myself—someone who is, first and foremost, a person. Someone who typically prefers the company of women and other people outside the gender binary, someone who likes talking about feelings and who prizes emotional intelligence and who likes to wear nail polish, and sometimes eyeliner too. I'm not saying I'm nothing like a man, or that the concept of manhood is so suffocatingly narrow that anyone who's not a beer-swilling all-American quarterback, with a gun in one hand and his raging boner in the other, couldn't possibly be a man. As it happens, I'm very much like a man in a number of different ways that have nothing to do with biology. I was assigned male at birth, and like I said in Chapter 13, I was socialized male. I still speak over women in conversation, though I try to catch myself. I still walk home alone at night comfortably without fearing being harassed or followed or worse. I still get treated with deference I don't necessarily deserve.

But I also get treated with suspicion I don't deserve either. I still find myself excluded from the kinds of conversations and interactions that I'd feel most at home in. Part of coming out as non-binary, for me, was pushing back against the Man Box and trying to signal to the world more clearly who I am inside, how I really feel. Because that's what gender is, on some level—giving the people around you a roadmap for how to interact with you, whether to call you "sir" or "ma'am" or something else, whether to buy you a drink or wait until you send one over. And when you're outside the clear cis binary that we all find so familiar, well, that map is a little less precise, and not as many people have a copy memorized. But more and more people are starting to understand the concept of non-binary people, and it's really not especially complicated. Even in the relatively narrow-minded North American culture, we've had terms for a long time for people who didn't quite fit into our views of gender—terms like "tomboy" and "mama's boy," for instance. Non-binary is an opportunity for the people who don't quite fit in to own the story of their not fitting in.

So I want to say, at this point in the book: If you've spent your life reckoning with a masculinity that didn't feel like it fit on you, then it's possible that you're not a man either. This book is not an attempt to "convert" cis kids to transness by any means. If you're a guy, you're a guy, and that's great. The world needs more men like you, people who are capable of reading through a whole book like this, of considering its points, of listening to new perspectives, men who are ready to grow into people who can change the world for the better.

But if you've ever felt, like I did increasingly as I made my way through my 20s, that the word "man" didn't exactly describe your gender, well, I want to encourage you to meditate on that—to consider why that is and what that might mean about you. It might be nothing, of course—but it also might be a sign that you're genderqueer in some way, and there's no harm in contemplating that possibility, exploring that idea. Talk to your friends about gender—about theirs and yours. Read about gender. Look into things like gender euphoria and gender dysphoria. This isn't that book, exactly—but it is for people like you too.

~

If you're still struggling with the last section, I understand. What gives me, someone who's not a man, the right to tell men how to be men? If you agree with me about my gender, then how is this any different from a woman writing such a book? When I came out, a friend of mine asked me to explain non-binariness to her. I told her it wasn't that the concept of being a man was so narrow that anything a little different made you not a man—it was whether you felt like a man inside, at your core. I told her there were definitely people who were less outwardly masculine than me who still identified wholly as men. But as someone who grew up as a boy and has worked writing for and about men all my adult life, I have a certain insight into what guys are going through right now, even if I don't count myself as one of them, and as someone who came out as non-binary in my 30s, I spent a lot of time wrestling with what being a man meant, how it felt and who it was for, analyzing it from as many angles as I could, like a jeweller appraising a diamond.

Gender is a lot more interesting than the black-and-white labels some people are keen to put on it. People so often compare human behaviour to animal behaviour in these situations, argue that because this or that member of the animal kingdom behaves in a certain way, it's a sign that we should, too. It strikes me as awfully intellectually timid to base your idea of how humans should organize society on what other animals do. Biology and gender may be in contact with each other, but they are far from the same thing, and gender is not static the way many people suppose. In his 1990 book *Manhood in the Making*, the anthropologist David Gilmore writes that in the various cultures he'd studied

> there is a constantly reoccurring notion that real manhood is different from simple anatomical male- ness, that it is not a natural condition that comes about spontaneously through biological matura- tion but rather is a precarious or artificial state that boys must win against powerful odds. This recur- rent notion that manhood is problematic, a critical threshold that boys must pass through testing, is found at all levels of sociocultural development

regardless of what other alternative roles are recognized. It is found among the simplest hunters
and fishermen, among peasants and sophisticated
urbanized peoples; it is found in all continents
and environments. It is found among both warrior
peoples and those who have never killed in anger.[146]

Addressing Gilmore's research in Boys Adrift, Leonard
Sax—who believes strongly in innate biological differences—writes that "the recurring theme is that 'culturally
defined competence . . . leads to reproductive success.'
In some cases, such as among traditional Orthodox Jews,
'culturally defined competence' is completely intellectual.
An Orthodox Jewish boy must prove his knowledge of
Torah and Talmud. In other cultures the travail is more
physical. But the underlying theme is the same."[147]

So what do we make of this? Though I take issue with
many of Sax's approaches to the topic of masculinity, I
think there's something hopeful in the note of similarity
between these two passages. Rather than suggesting that
there's one single way to be a man, the two quotes imply
that manhood is one thing towards which there are many
paths. But even with a myriad of paths, I think it's important
to remember that you don't have to take any of those paths
if you don't want to. Recognizing that can be immensely

146   David D. Gilmore, *Manhood in the Making: Cultural
Concepts of Masculinity* (New Haven: Yale University Press, 1990).
147   Leonard Sax, *Boys Adrift : The Five Factors Driving the
Growing Epidemic of Unmotivated Boys and Underachieving Young
Men* (New York: Basic Books, 2007).

freeing. There's a whole wide world out there. As the meme goes, "Which way, Western man?" But rather than two options, there are infinite ones.

The one thing you should do is choose carefully. Because the culture around you is changing, and sticking to the same old tired scripts that worked for your grandfather or your father is unlikely to bring you the same rewards. Change is needed. It's time for men to reinvent themselves, individually and as a group. If you look at contemporary masculinity and see a mass of people resistant to change—and it's hard not to, sometimes—there is hope. When I get stuck thinking like that, I come back to Steve Biddulph's thoughts on this from *The New Manhood*: "There is one outstanding piece of evidence for a massive change being possible—women have already done it."

"In just four decades from the early 1970s to the present, and against fierce opposition," he writes, "an entire gender has redefined itself. The Women's Movement overturned thousands of years of oppression and restriction, an unprecedented and historic shift. When the human race *needs* to change, it can do so very fast."[148]

That was one of my aims in writing this book—to provide a guide for the boys and men who were faced with this wave of change, who were feeling daunted by the foundations of gender shifting below their feet. Because so many of the books about masculinity out there don't offer much for the young male reader, the teen boy or young man at the cusp of his real life beginning. That's

---

148   Biddulph, *The New Manhood*.

especially galling, I think, because so many of these same books suggest those are the people who need the most guidance, and, as I discussed in the introduction, they're people who are often a little bit adrift, unmoored from the fabric of society at large.

Two of the books I read, and have cited on multiple occasions throughout this book, did include a set of guidelines in their final chapters: *Raising Cain*, by Dan Kindlon and Michael Thompson, and *The Decline of Men*, by Guy Garcia. The former was advice for people raising boys, and the latter advice for men themselves, but between the two, a sort of synthesis emerged. Both preached the importance of vulnerability, the importance of character-building, the importance of connecting. And both ended, I felt, on hopeful notes about the value of self-expression and being your own self: "Teach boys that there are many ways to be a man,"[149] says the former, and "Don't follow The Rules,"[150] says the latter.

~

It's a running joke of sorts among people who live outside of cis gender roles, whether they're non-binary or trans, genderqueer or genderfluid, bi-gender, agender or anything else, that talking about gender with cis people, especially cishet men, is an exercise in painful futility.

These conversations aren't just painfully futile because cis people so often enter into these conversations with

---

149 Kindlon and Thompson, *Raising Cain*.
150 Garcia, *The Decline of Men*.

hurtful prejudices, with transphobia, with intent to injure—
though it's also this, of course—but because perhaps even
more often, cis people simply have no idea what they're
talking about in these conversations.

One particular meme about this fact sticks in my mind—
"talking about gender with trans people" is represented
by a painting of Greek philosophers expounding; "talking
about gender with cis people" is represented by a picture
of an adult showing a toy to a toddler.

It's an apt comparison, sadly. Even the most well-
meaning cis people often have about as much experience
thinking deeply about gender as a two-year-old has with
high-school math. Which makes sense—to be cis, in a
sense, is to be someone who lives their life without having
to think about gender. When you're born into a body that's
assigned a gender that conforms with the gender you feel
most comfortable with, you've got an easy job ahead of
you. There's no force pushing or pulling you to think
more deeply about what a boy thing is, who separates boy
things from girl things or what it means if a boy wants to
try out some of the girl things. But as we've seen earlier
in this book, not thinking about things is often a shortcut
to thinking—and acting—badly. To being cruel, to being
shortsighted. When rules and laws governing trans and
non-binary people are written and conceived by people
who don't think about gender very much, or very deeply,
you end up with unfair situations at best and nightmarish
state-backed transphobia at worst. That's what we see in
the wave of anti-trans bills and laws that swept America
in 2022, when I was first writing this conclusion.

The tragedy of this, of course, is it means that the world is not short of opportunities where strength and power, properly applied, can make a difference for good. Whatever it looks like when I call for men to try to wear makeup or cry openly, this book isn't a call for you to pivot to a self-effacing and fey demeanour. Above all, it's a call to pivot the content instead of the delivery. It's a call to recognize which situations call for that familiar, old-school bravado and machismo and which ones call for flexibility, thoughtfulness and listening. I'm not saying never interrupt anyone, I'm saying interrupt homophobes. I'm not saying don't talk over anyone, I'm saying talk over anti-vaxxers. I'm not saying don't invade anyone's personal space, I'm saying invade the personal space of street harassers. Intimidate bullies. Threaten abusers. Beat up fascists. If you're going to be a man's man, be one for good.

It would be hypocritical of me to tell you that there is no value to old-school masculinity, nothing to be gained from looking, being or acting tough. This book is not an attempt to scrub from you or anyone every last trace of what we might call machismo, manliness or masculinity. No matter how tough you feel on the inside, there will be times in your life where acting like a man is necessary, useful or important. What I'm advocating for is the recognition that gender is something we choose, and as such masculinity is just a mode that you can flip to and away from when the situation calls for it. Being able to recognize that "acting like a man" is a choice can open your eyes to the fact that in some situations, it's a good choice and in some situations, it's a bad choice. Contemporary views on gender too often to seek to clamp down on this approach, insisting that gender is sex, that sex is biology, that biology is destiny. This is not only scientifically unsound, it's also incredibly reductive and leads to unhealthy outcomes for everyone involved. It's time for us to collectively recognize that gender is something we do, not something we are; that it can change, evolve, cycle in and out like seasons. Armed with this knowledge, you can recognize that the useful, important and meaningful aspects of masculinity are a tool in your toolbox, not the beginning and end of who you are.

Just because you can't be the cowboy on the screen doesn't mean you can't act anything like him—you just have to recognize that the bravery and power he and his ilk embodied onscreen were marshalled in service of a bigoted worldview, one that was accepted by broad swaths of North American society at the time, but is no longer. But being stereotyped based on your gender is nothing new. For much of human history, women were tasked with the unhappy burden of teaching their daughters the unfairness of being a woman, the way their lives would be ones of physical pain, of fear, of subservience.

Years from now, men may just have to do something similar for their sons. Maybe they'll have to teach their sons that being a man is difficult, that it isn't an enviable position—that they'll have to work harder to be accepted, that their humanity might be called into question, that they'll miss out on opportunities just because they're men. Maybe these fathers will have to reiterate that there's nothing wrong with being a man, that men can do anything if they set their minds to it. And if they do, they'll be right—because just like women and queer people, men can be hardworking, creative, loving people; good friends and talented lovers; pillars of a community, trustworthy neighbours. Men can love, and be loved, and do things they'll be remembered for, whether that's making their mark on history, or simply taking the time to be there for the people they care about.

~

Back to the stairs. You might be wondering: what the hell does climbing the stairs have to do with masculinity? That's a fair question, and we'll get to it in due course.

For starters, it's worth remembering that however physical, however solid your body feels—being made, as it is, of bone enveloped in flesh; the way it can impact the world, for instance if ever you've thrown and landed a punch—it is not an object but a series of little miracles, an alchemy of chemical reactions in progress.

The littlest thing going wrong, the smallest remainder to an equation, can end it all in a heartbeat, for one; for two, what your body is is a vehicle for a consciousness, where both car and driver are forever in flux. It's said that you cannot set foot in the same stream twice, but it's rarely remembered that the foot you're setting in those streams is changing too.

In the end, the two months I spent climbing the stairs instead of taking the elevator laid bare the fiction that the body is static. Every week or so the same stairs I'd climbed seemed shorter, easier to conquer. But I knew it was me who was changing, not them.

As I grew more comfortable with them, I began experimenting. I'd try to take them two at a time, and see how fast I could do it. Then back to one at a time and seeing how steady I could keep my breathing, how low my heart rate.

Then I'd try to push past the eighth floor and see how high I could go. Eventually I was doing the whole building in one shot, ground floor to 14th. Then I started doing the whole building twice a day. Then three times. Then four. At one point I stepped into the stairwell, took a breath, and started jogging upward.

The truisms were true, after all: a long journey does begin with a single step.

The connection I see between taking the stairs or the elevator is this: contemporary masculinity is sort of like an elevator. It's a means to an end, a way to get somewhere quickly and conveniently, one that millions and millions of men take every day without thinking too much about it. But because it's the easy way to get there, it's also at odds with the more traditional ideal of masculinity, that you become a man by testing yourself, by doing things the hard way, by mastering something difficult.

In buying into this mentality, men, it strikes me, are always taking the easy way out. They're conforming to an ideal that doesn't exactly fit them, that's not good for them or anyone else, because they're afraid of being criticized. And if they were to take the metaphorical stairs—if they were to step outside the Man Box—some of those criticisms might very well come their way. But those criticisms, however much they might sting, are never spoken with your best intentions at heart. They're crabs in a bucket, all trying to pull the other crabs back down so nobody can escape.

Doing difficult things—taking the path less travelled—comes slowly at first. But if you stick with it, you become someone else, the way someone exercising day in and day out changes as a physical body.

In the beginning, breaking the rules might not be easy. But who ever felt proud of themselves just for taking the easy route every morning?

If you enjoyed this book,
please consider passing it—
or the things you learned from it—
on to a young man in your life.

acknowledgements

Thank you to Carly Watters, my awesome agent, for believing in me and this book, for all the heavy lifting you did on this project—and for the title, of course. Signing with you felt life-changing, and in a way, now it is.

Thank you to Pia Singhal (and the team at ECW) for believing in this book when many others didn't, for seeing what I saw, and for helping it be the best version of itself, from the big-picture structural changes to all the tiny line edits. Having someone smart, passionate and wise in my camp was invaluable and made all the scary parts feel manageable. And thank you to my copy editor, Jen Knoch, and my fact checker, Angelina Mazza, for your thorough and thoughtful work.

(Thank you also to Haley Cullingham—this book's moment of conception was an email from you. Your interest in it when it was just an idea of mine helped make it real, and your investment and reassurance even when it didn't stick right away were enormously helpful. And to Rick Meier and David Ross, your interest, too, kept me aloft.)

Thank you to Emma McKay—my time at AskMen was unbelievably important in forming the ideas that would go on to become this book. Thank you for seeing my potential, and nurturing it.

Thank you to my friends, too numerous to name. Your love, care and jokes helped keep me sane during this process.

Thank you to my family—Frank, Diana and Nathalie. You made me who I am; this book would not be what it is without you. And to Sandra and Paul, for your counsel and wisdom.

Most of all, thank you to Blair, my love, my prickly pear.

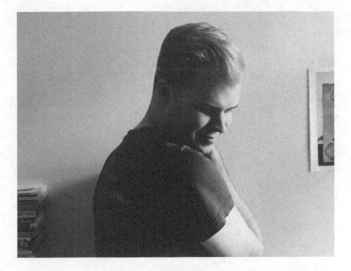

Alex Manley is a Montreal-based editor, translator, and award-winning writer who has worked for AskMen since 2013, and whose work has been published by *Hazlitt*, *The Walrus*, *Vulture*, *Catapult*, *Electric Literature*, *Maisonneuve* magazine, and *THIS* magazine, among others.

This book is also available as a Global Certified Accessible™ (GCA) ebook. ECW Press's ebooks are screen reader friendly and are built to meet the needs of those who are unable to read standard print due to blindness, low vision, dyslexia or a physical disability.

At ECW Press, we want you to enjoy our books in whatever format you like. If you've bought a print copy just send an email to ebook@ecwpress.com and include:

- the book title
- the name of the store where you purchased it
- a screenshot or picture of your order/receipt number and your name
- your preference of file type: PDF (for desktop reading), ePub (for a phone/tablet, Kobo, or Nook), mobi (for Kindle)

A real person will respond to your email with your ebook attached. Please note this offer is only for copies bought for personal use and does not apply to school or library copies.

Thank you for supporting an independently owned Canadian publisher with your purchase!

This book is made of paper from well-managed FSC® - certified forests, recycled materials, and other controlled sources.

 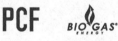